"Marjorie Jackson does an amazing job of articulating exciting Bible stories with the desire to challenge and motivate readers to dig into God's Word!"

—**MICHELLE DUGGAR**, Mother of TLC's *19 Kids and Counting*

"Marjorie Jackson is a lovely young lady who radiates joy and grace, and walks in wisdom beyond her years. In *The Greatest Book You've Never Read* she leads young (and not-so-young) readers on a delightful journey to the very source of that joy, grace, and wisdom—a simple love for God and a passion for His Word!"

—**TWILA PARIS**, Christian music artist

"Marjorie Jackson has a style that is both warm and wise. She's an encouraging writer who will help your faith grow and a new friend you'll enjoy spending time with too. Find a few quiet moments each day to spend with her book and your life will never be the same!"

—**HOLLEY GERTH**, Best-selling author of *You're Already Amazing*

The Greatest Book You've Never Read
Why the Bible is not only exciting, but it will change your life!

ISBN 978-1-4675-9502-5

Edited by Tessa Swehla and Jennifer Hutchins
Designed by ThinkpenDesign.com with Marjorie Jackson
Illustrated & Typeset by Marjorie Jackson
Author Photo: Greg Jackson

I dedicate this book firstly to my beloved Heavenly Father, whose love has never failed me and will never fail me. You are the One who gives me the words to write. Thank you for choosing me as your vessel; all the glory goes *solely* to You!

And secondly, I dedicate this book to my earthly father—my amazing, loving, hard-working daddy, Greg Jackson. This book would be an impossibility without your careful guidance in all things design, typesetting, layout, and even content. But more importantly, you encouraged and empowered me throughout this project and I am more than grateful. I'm sure you'll find a few of the lessons I've learned from you sprinkled into this book. I love you both!

The GREATEST BOOK

{N} You've Ever Read ↓

Why the BIBLE is not only EXCITING, but it will CHANGE YOUR LIFE!

 MARJORIE JACKSON

Table of Contents

Introduction

Easier Said than Done

eep! Beep!

You groan and pull a pillow over your head as your alarm clock sounds at 5:00 a.m. Groggily sliding out of bed, you make an attempt to navigate to your desk, despite the blurry vision of your eyes, which are snapping shut every two seconds.

As you take a seat (or slouch) at your desk, you let out a thunderous yawn and aimlessly flail your arms in the direction of your neat leather Bible, resting at the peak of a stack of books. As you pull the Book towards you, another booming yawn releases. You haven't been this tired in months.

You decide to read whichever portion of the Bible you flip to first. Closing your eyes (which doesn't take much effort), you run your fingers on the continuous golden edges of the pages, opening to a section at random. You cautiously open your eyes and behold the chapter your unsystematic method chose for you—Leviticus 2.

"When someone brings a grain offering to the Lord, his offering is to be of fine flour." You blink drowsily. "He is to pour oil on it, put incense on it..." Your eyes are open halfway and you let out a yawn. "...and take it to Aaron's sons the priests." That's it. You collapse asleep, absolutely limp with exhaustion, face square in the middle of Leviticus.

———————————————————————

Maybe you had an experience similar to the one above. I know I've had similar experiences (I'm *not* a morning person). Perhaps you heard a great speaker or missionary talk about their relationship with God and how their whole Christian lifestyle pivoted off of their daily quiet time spent deep in the Word prior to daybreak. Inspired, you may have resolved to be an early riser in order to read an entire book of the Bible each day. Then, when morning rolled around, your energy was not quite as passionate as your inspiration. In fact, you probably began to dread Bible reading, because, let's face it— we think it's boring. Maybe you're looking for the key to being able to grab your Bible and read it without drowning in boredom.

The Bible is one of the ways God speaks to us; it's like His handwritten Letter to His beloved children (that would be us!). Committing time each day to read God's Letter to us is one of the most important, precious, and valuable decisions that we'll ever make, considering how essential it is to growing in our relationship with God. However, to read the Bible just to check it off our to-do lists or without understanding or growing in the Lord is like chewing our food to please our parents, but spitting it out when they walk out of the room.

You might be thinking, *But it's boring!* Well, if you're reading about grain offerings in Leviticus, you may be biting off more than you can chew for the time being. Carving time out of even the most stressful of days to read the Bible is meant to strengthen your faith and relationship with the one-and-only Most High God, but if you don't think about the verses you read and apply them, then they are just meaningless letters assembled together neatly on a page. And if the Bible was just that, then it wouldn't be so important to waste our time reading and studying it. But no, it is so much more.

Through this book, I want you to realize what an amazing Book we have access to. We have a marvelous work of literature and riveting stories. We have astoundingly accurate accounts of the beginning to the end of the history of the earth. We have been mailed a letter from the perfect, loving Father who brought us into being. And, we have also been handed a manual to life (For a second there, you probably thought I was talking about this book!). Understanding, meditating, and reading the Bible daily is so, so important and crucial for those of us seeking to truly commit ourselves to our Savior and to live the life God has in store for us, that I can hardly press the fact enough.

SPIRITUAL STARVATION

Has it ever happened that you are lying in your bed at the end of a long day at the end of a long week, not quite asleep yet and silently thinking to yourself, when all of a sudden you realize something— you forgot to eat *all* week!...again! Man, *that* really slipped your mind. Oh well, at least tomorrow you'll eat your scheduled Sunday morning family breakfast—it is a tradition, after all. You usually nibble on a light breakfast: a little pancake, half a stick of bacon, and, if you have room, a donut hole or two. The rest of the week, you usually forget to eat because you're so busy, and you just don't have the time. If you *do* happen to remember, you fish a cold french fry out of a box of leftovers, and just leave it at that.

You may be thinking, *What?! This is completely unrealistic. How do you* forget *to eat?!* The truth is, this example isn't so far-fetched. True, we couldn't go a week without physical food and *not* acknowledge tremendous pains and symptoms that our bodies send us, because our bodies need that food to live. Yet, as unrealistic as it sounds, the majority of proclaimed Christians on earth follow this pattern. No, no… they eat the food on their dinner plates. Their stomachs growl and hunger pains flood in if they don't. But what slips their minds is their *spiritual food.* What is spiritual food? It's the nourishment we get from reading the Word. It's like vitamins for our spirit. It's *reading the Bible.* Someone might go to church for two hours on Sunday mornings, but how is anybody whose spirit longs for a real relationship with God supposed to withstand such terrible starvation time and time again?

Whether it's an active school, sports, work, or social life that prevents designated meal times to fill the spiritual food tank, Bible reading doesn't seem to take high priority as its rank. Yeah, we have a spiritual breakfast on Sunday mornings, but look at it this way: If, out of the seven days in a week, we starve for six days and eat on the seventh, how is our health going to be affected? For better or for worse? Hands down, our health is going to plummet to the floor. We'll be as skinny as wires and as transparent as glasses of water… if even that. You don't suppose the 'spiritual person' of an inconsistent Bible reader could look like this miserable and famished being? I wonder.

Okay… well if the Bible is so crucial to our spiritual homeostasis, what are we getting out of it? *How*, exactly, is it a crucial element to a firm walk with the Lord? Well, for starters, it is one of the main ways God talks to us. We may not hear an earth-shaking, ear-splitting heavenly voice when communicating with the Lord, but He definitely speaks through His Letter to us. Words often jump off the pages at us, screaming *"THIS FITS YOUR SITUATION!"* or *"THIS IS WHAT GOD THINKS OF YOU!"* or *"THIS IS THE ANSWER!"* Really, God can say anything through His Word. One of the unique things about the Bible is that the verses can mean different things to different people at different times! There is so much meaning, because there is so much God wants to tell so many people! When we take the time to understand and process the words we read in a passage, we grow in that area, because it is on our minds and in our hearts. Reading the Bible and taking it to heart will improve the way you live your life— it says so, right in Psalm 119:11, "I have hidden your word in my heart, that I might not sin against you."

There's no need to feel like an evil person if you don't find much excitement or true, applicable meaning in the Bible yet. You are about to discover an amazing gift you've had all along that you haven't opened yet! Today is the day of the birth of a fresh new excitement about the Holy Bible—so go ahead, don't wait 'til Christmas: unwrap it!

BIBLICAL BLOCKBUSTER

Have you ever had the urge to read a well-written, engrossing novel... perhaps an action-packed, fast paced adventure? Look no further than the Bible! From escaping a cruel life of slavery to battling a raging giant to surviving an inconvenient shipwreck (but, then again, when *are* shipwrecks convenient?), the stories in

God's Word are better than a movie! Like movies, there are genres galore in the Bible: one for everyone and everything.

I may sound like I am practically flat on my face begging you to read the Word each day, but the truth is, this decision of yours isn't affecting me. I may never know if you decide to make this awesome choice (although, I would love to hear if you do or if you have made that decision! Contact me!), but the Lord sure will, and you'll reap the benefits. This is a decision that solely revolves around you and your relationship with God.

What are the benefits, you ask? Dear reader, this is merely an introduction to an entire book listing benefit after benefit! You'll grow in your relationship with the Lord, you'll discover truth, meaning, and answers to questions, you'll be encouraged, your living will improve, you will hear (er, read) God's voice, and so much more! Find out for yourself: pick up the Bible and begin reading. I'd recommend starting in one of the gospels (Matthew, Mark, Luke, and John) if you are a new Bible reader or new Christian. The gospels are the foundation for our Christian faith, and it will really give you a solid reason to *want* to strengthen your relationship with God.

Hopefully it won't take too long before you realize the meaning and power of the selfless life of Jesus Christ! And that's only four out of sixty-six books in the Bible. You're in for a treat! I hope that by the end of this book, you'll be discovering the Bible and growing spiritually on your own as you dive into the expert Work of the Most High God.

In many books, one of the first pages may say something like, "Dedicated to my dear Aunt Betsie, who has been my inspiration though the years" or, "To my kids, who never cease to encourage me and brighten up my day!" While you probably won't find a dedication in the front of your Bible, you will find one throughout the entire *Book*. And who has the Author (God), dedicated this incredible book to? *You.* He penned all sixty-six books with *you* in mind. He knew, before He made you or the world, that you would have troubles in life and that you wouldn't be perfect. He knew (and knows) everything about you.

God's Book is also dedicated to me…and to your brother… and to your next-door-neighbor…and to your dentist. One amazing aspect about the Bible is that although it is for everyone, it is just as personal as though it had been written for only you. God knows everyone, and then He knows *only you.* If that doesn't make you feel loved and wanted, then what does?!

God compiled some of His powerful works and events in history and arrayed them in a Book for us to refer to in any situation in life. Whatever the situation concerns, there is a solution in the Bible. See how Joseph forgave his brothers for selling him—here is the answer to the conflict with our siblings. Proverbs has solid advice on watching the words that you say—here's the key to not saying things so often that we'll regret. Browse Paul's letters for tips on living a selfless, loving life—we won't have to search very far. See what I mean? If there were a dedication at the beginning of the Bible, it would probably look something like this: "To my beloved child, [your name here]. I love you more than you could ever imagine." And He really, truly means it!

In this life, neither you nor I will *ever* understand everything about the Bible or God, but we should learn as much as we can. Don't hesitate any longer—open up the Book dedicated to you and digest the spiritual food that you, perhaps unknowingly, are so hungrily craving. Believe me, the Bible is The Greatest Book You've Never Read!

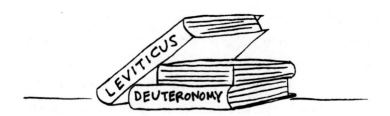

CHAPTER 1
I'm Bored

FIRST IMPRESSIONS

Sixty-six books collecting dust on a bookshelf sat hopelessly squashed between the newest and greatest hit novel and a pile of DVDs. The books, on the outside, were tattered and caked in a layer of dust frosting. The deceitful boredom of the appearance kept others from lifting them off the shelf to read the important content. Nobody could tell, and nobody seemed to care. The truth is, not many knew. The full potential of this collection remained unknown, year after year.

The door flung open and powerfully rammed into the wall, causing particles of sheetrock to fly in every which direction... and causing all sixty-six books to tumble to the floor. Four siblings ran into the room with three empty boxes, some wet rags, and a duster.

"Spring cleaning!" one boy's voice rang out melodiously. Tearing into the bookshelf, the four siblings pulled off book after DVD after video game, and tossed them into one of their three boxes: a trash box, a donate box, and an attic storage box. In a matter of minutes, the shelf looked like a bare wasteland: except for the floor, where the sixty-six books remained.

"Should we keep these books?" The youngest asked the rest.

"Nah, they're boring." It was unanimous. Although they had never actually read or understood the books, everyone agreed that those books looked dry and uninteresting.

"Which pile should they go in?"

With a nod, they agreed, "The attic." As the decision, again, was unanimous, they tossed all sixty-six books in the dull cardboard box without any second thoughts.

THE REAL DEAL

Did someone say, "Boring?" Hold on… Are we talking about the same Bible here? Sadly, yes. Many people have the sad misconception that, as much as we don't like to admit that we think so, perhaps the Bible is a boring, irrelevant, judgmental book for pious adults or pastors. Even those who have never thought those things have felt them: when time comes to open the Bible and read, a secret dread creeps over them as they flip through the seemingly daunting Book. Why do we think these things about the Bible, God's Word? Was it something someone said? Has culture or media forced us to believe that God's Word is lifeless? Is it the fact that we don't see the Bible as containing anything interesting or important? These are all valid possibilities… yet the myth remains: The Bible is boring. What do we do? Let's bust this myth once and for all: The Bible is not boring. The Bible is for you! *Who me?* Yes, you!

The Bible is a good deal: sixty-six books for the price of one, not to mention that it has multiple uses (no, I don't mean that it can be used as a decoration, placemat, or a doorstopper). For example, as a storybook alone, the Bible contains a broad variety of great story lines. Don't agree? Part of the problem may be that you aren't getting the full-color, professional acting version of the story playing in your imagination. Perhaps you picture jolly, pink-cheeked old Noah standing in front of an ark with two bright yellow giraffes happily boarding, along with some purple elephants and some smiling zebras. Then, a little drip-drop of rain trickles on to the ark—Noah's cue to pull out his umbrella!

Do you honestly think that's how Noah's story went? I think that's how the preschool Sunday school lesson went! Don't let the children's Bibles paint the visuals for Bible stories. Children's Bibles are great for starting a solid, Christian foundation in the first few years of someone's life, but now, as young people seeking to know more about God and His Word, we should venture on to read and know the real thing. The Bible, like movies, music, and literature, is full of different genres. You'll find action, adventure, love, tragedy, poetry, and so much more between the covers.

Some of the greatest stories in the Bible are the powerful stories of Jesus Christ. Nothing compares with reading about God's son, the man who gave His life for us so that we have the hope of salvation. It is humbling to really think about what He did for us. His unending love and His heart touch the lives of people everywhere. The many stories of His life on earth are not just for us to read about, say "Wow, that's great!" and walk away only to forget what we just read, but they're a perfect standard for us to compare our own lives to. In order to imitate Christ, as 1 Corinthians 11:1 says to do, we need to know what He was like and who He was. The Bible, as you may have already guessed, is the perfect place to acquire information about God's Son.

LOVE TO KNOW MORE?

One of the major genres discussed in the Bible is love. Love? Maybe the idea of love sounds gross to you… or, maybe you think it sounds great. Don't jump to conclusions too soon! While romantic love does come up in the Bible, it is only one of many different departments in the love category. As young people, romantic love is probably not the first thing on our minds. *Well, what other kind of love is there?* The word love is often times thought of and used in the context of romance, but the Bible proves that love has many other meanings.

Yeah, there is some romance, because the Bible is for everyone, and there is a time and place to be reading about those things. It is good to know what God says, commands, and requires on the subject, even as a young person who won't be thinking about marriage or romance for some time. We need to know where we stand in our beliefs, and what we consider right and wrong, because, especially nowadays, the world is trying to fill people, especially youth, with wrong, impure, and sinful views on subjects such as love and marriage. Of course, don't rush ahead of the game: take in God's views about romantic things in the Bible in age-appropriate levels and doses (this being said, maybe postpone joining the Song of Solomon Bible study).

The Bible contains all things A-Z on love. The NLT Bible mentions the word "love" 763 times. The Bible is written by Love! How is that possible, you ask? Read 1 John 4:8 for the answer. *Is love that big a deal?* Yes! Many Bible stories are love stories—not romantic love stories, but true love stories. Name one and there's a good chance it's about love: It could be about brotherly love (like Miriam watching baby Moses as he drifted down the river in a basket). Or maybe, it's about love for friends (like Jonathan helping David hide in a cave from the crazy and infuriated King Saul). Perhaps the story emphasizes love for God and His Son (disciples leaving everything to follow Jesus). The story may be about God's love for us (God sending his Son to die for our sins). The Bible revolves on the topic of love (more on love in chapter 4)!

OUR FIELD GUIDE TO LIFE

Sure, the Bible has great stories and literary masterpieces, but there is so much more to the Bible than that. God didn't write the Bible to entertain us or for us to read once and shove into a bookshelf to collect dust. We ultimately look to the Bible to teach us the way to live. In fact, it's the perfect place to look, considering that the Author, God, created living. God sent His Son, Jesus, to live on the earth for thirty-three years, and Jesus was an expert at living. God's Word is packed to the brim with pointers on living life right.

Life differs from person to person—maybe your life isn't so hard right now. As young people, we have a tendency to take things for granted—like the brussels sprouts we secretly spit out into our napkin, the boring car rides we have to endure when visiting our out-of-state family members, and maybe the Wi-Fi that goes haywire now and then. Sometimes it seems like the only thing we lack is the one gadget we didn't get for Christmas.

Or, maybe your life feels like an uphill mountain trek—painful, sharp blasts of frigid wind, rocky cliffs, deep pitfalls and crevices— in other words, maybe your life is hard. Maybe you truly feel hurt and lost, and you'd like a clue in which direction to go or something/someone comforting to cling to. In this world, spiritual directions aren't very clear—many find themselves standing at crossroads, with arrows pointing in every which direction.

Whichever description you feel fits your life right now best, there are still things we need to know and practice as a way of life, whether we're eight, eighteen, fifty-eight, or one hundred eight. And whether life gets hard or life is hard already, there is one place to turn. Overflowing with answers to every problem imaginable, it would be appropriate to call the Bible our field guide to life. From watching our words to not being worried to being thankful to exercising self-control to loving our neighbor as ourselves, there is Scripture that applies for everyone.

Look back at those examples; surely, you've struggled with all of those before. Maybe you've made a less-than-polite remark to your sister when she took your bike for a ride without permission. Perhaps you've worried that others will mock you for your beliefs. Did you ever receive a thoughtful gift from your grandma that you couldn't find anything positive about (like the time she bought you a sweater with a soccer ball embroidered on it... since she knew you liked playing soccer, she assumed you'd like wearing it, too)? Or what about a time when you're at a friend's house, and they have the dreaded idea of watching the movie forbidden by your parents? Maybe you know someone who's a little, um, difficult to show kindness to? Everyone's faced trials of the sort. So yes, the Bible addresses our everyday issues, as well.

Paul's letters to the early churches are just as valid to us as they were to those who preceded us by nearly two thousand years. His epistles are instant favorites with those who need guidance in their life on all things...well, life!

Another great place to look for applicable pointers on living a godly, stable life is Proverbs, full of bite-sized, flavorful chunks of solid, sensible advice. You should try to read a proverb a day. Chew, blow, smack, and chomp on it like a piece of gum that never loses flavor. In other words, meditate on it. By meditate I mean thinking about what the verse means, and how you can personally put that into action in your life as a young person. Just think and apply—that's exactly how real Bible reading is done. Doing this regularly is going to grow you spiritually like eating vegetables will grow you physically. Of course, if you're like me (not an avid vegetable fan), you will probably like Bible reading *much* better. Your faith and beliefs will be rooted in solid ground and unshakeable if you read, believe, and know the Word.

Our Life Manual

Just like cars come with manuals that are loaded with information concerning everything and anything we ever want (or don't want) to know about the vehicles, life also came with a Manual (hint, hint—the Bible). This Manual that God has given us doesn't just tell us how to fix problems, but it tells how to prevent problems and how to use things. The Bible basically tells us about our "gauges."

Our talents, thoughts, words, personalities, and such are kind of like our "gauges." God has given us each a unique dashboard. The Manual makes life a lot clearer. We can avoid lots of car trouble by taking a peek at the car manual; and, sure enough, we can avoid heaps of life trouble by opening the Life Manual.

What does the Manual say about the purpose of our many gauges? In 1 Corinthians 10:13 it specifically says "…whatever you do, do it all for the glory of God." So, our gauges serve the purpose of glorifying God. There we have it! Just like a speedometer's purpose is to tell what speed the car is going, and a gas level serves the purpose of showing how much gasoline is in the tank, our gauges should bring glory to God.

The Manual also covers another aspect of life—our "special features". Sometimes, a car will have a seat warming option, automatic closing doors, or headphones and a DVD player. Our Manual informs us about our special features, too. In 1 Corinthians 2:16, Paul advertises one of our exciting special features: "…we have the mind of Christ." Whoa! That is huge. The mind of Christ? A fully pure, sinless mind!

You may be wondering, *How is that so? I'm a Christian, but I still think sinful thoughts sometimes. Sometimes I judge others, sometimes I think rebellious thoughts, and sometimes my mind is just plain idle!* It is possible to never use the seat warming option, or to never watch a movie in the car or use the headphones. It is also possible to never use the mind of Christ (or any other special feature) we've been given. The special features that God has installed in His children, those who have accepted Jesus as their Savior, are far better than automatic closing doors. We get the mind of Christ, we are the temple of God's Holy Spirit who's living in us (1 Corinthians 3:16), and we are more than conquerors through Jesus Christ (Romans 8:37).

The Manual also gives us the Lord's commands and tells us to follow them. It tells us things not to do, as well. It is not giving us a pointless list of "do's and don'ts," but it is rather guiding us through God's loving instructions that He gives us in order to help us live a God-centered life. Not to mention, His commands are in our best interest, even when they don't seem like it.

For instance, your parents probably taught you at an early age that sticking your finger in an electrical outlet is a very bad idea. You may not have been too pleased with their command at the time... in fact, my three-year-old sister gave a pretty good scream at the reprimand she got for sticking a shoelace in the outlet (do not try this at home, either). Now, of course, I'm sure you see the wisdom and point of their restriction. They obviously were not thinking, *Oh boy, let's keep our kids from having fun with the electric outlet by telling them to not stick their fingers inside of it!* That would be ridiculous. Their reason was because they truly cared and looked out for you.

Once we realize the purpose, even more do we appreciate the regulations our parents lovingly set for us, because they're set to keep us safe—physically, spiritually, mentally, and emotionally. Same with God's instructions—He tells us not to be prideful, because "pride goes before destruction..." (Proverbs 16:18). Thanks to God's instructions, we don't have to go before destruction, or discover tough life lessons by ruining our lives. We can simply obey the Manual.

WHAT'S HE SAYING?

Have you ever heard God speak to you? Maybe you haven't heard Him speak by an audible human voice, but He talks to us more than we realize. *Well, God did speak out loud to the prophet Samuel, so why not me?* We have to understand that it is God's choice on how He wants to speak and reveal Himself to us. Are we using all of our listening senses? Our ears may not hear anything, but what about our hearts? Your heart can hear the "still, small voice"—the Holy Spirit of God speaking to us.

One of the many times we may hear that voice is during Bible reading. For example, you may read, "You must each decide in your heart how much to give. And don't give reluctantly or in response to pressure. 'For God loves a person who gives cheerfully,'" in 2 Corinthians 9:7. God may whisper in his still, small voice to you that He appreciates the joyful gift you gave out of your savings in the church missions offering, and He may speak by just letting you feel a sense of encouragement and love. God's still, small voice isn't restricted to just words—feelings, while they can be misleading at times, can also be from God. Of course, never put it beyond God to boom a resounding, audible voice to speak to you. It's fully up to Him.

Now… what if we can't understand the Bible?

Well, to begin with, there are different versions of the Bible. Some families stick straight to one version of the Bible, while others read from an array of versions. The decision of which Bible version to read from is ultimately between you and your parents. Some versions are easier than others, so if you find the version you're reading to be difficult, you may want to check with your parents to see if they have another version that they would allow you to read, possibly relieving you of any confusing terminology. Respect your parents' choice about any version. After all, no matter which one you use, you'll still find Ephesians 6:1-3 there, still commanding all young people to obey and honor their parents.

Besides multiple versions, there are other resources that can assist us with our understanding of the verses we read. In the case of difficult words, Mr. Noah Webster comes through to help us—use a dictionary! Thesauruses can be helpful as well. No, that's not over the top, it's going above and beyond to understand God's Word! A devotional would be a helpful guide to Bible reading times. Ask your parents if they know of a trusted commentary on the passage you are trying to understand. Better yet, ask a trusted, godly, Christian adult, like a parent or pastor, to help you understand what you're reading by explaining it to you.

Ultimately, prayer is the best resort when you can't understand the Bible. Ask God to give you understanding and to show you what the verses mean. We can pray to God about anything at all. He is our Friend and Father once Jesus is our Savior and Lord; we can speak to Him plainly. Everyone loves it when their friends take time to talk to them, and of course, the Lord is no exception! God loves it when we talk to Him!

I hope you are as excited as I am to dive into the amazing Word of God, which is sharper than the sharpest two-edged sword (Hebrews 4:12). To end each chapter, there will be a challenge and a set of discussion questions to explore your thoughts about the topics. I hope that you develop a strong love for the true Word of the Lord, and for God Himself! By reading His Word and applying it, you will see a notable, favorable difference in your walk with God. What could be more exciting than a relationship with the King of kings, Lord of lords, and Creator of the earth? He is, by far, the ultimate Best Friend. The beginning to a fresh, new relationship with our Heavenly Father through His Holy Word starts... NOW!

I DARE YOU...

If you have not formed a habit of daily Bible reading, today is your day to start! Find a time where you can spend five minutes reading the Bible—set a timer if you have to! We make time to eat, sleep, and have fun, so let's make some time to eat our spiritual food. Maybe before or after school? While you eat? Listen to it on audio while doing your chores? Maybe you could keep a Bible in the restroom! Just make it your goal to spend at least five minutes a day in the Word. You won't regret it.

If you have formed a habit of daily Bible reading, today is your day to continue! How about trying to memorize some Scripture? It is important to fill our minds with the Word of God. It's not so hard to memorize verses. After all, we memorize songs, movie/TV lines, math facts, theater lines, and Dr. Seuss books nearly everyday, whether we realize it or not! Here are a few suggestions to start with: Psalm 23:1, Proverbs 1:7, John 3:16, Romans 12:21, Philippians 4:8, Hebrews 11:1, James 4:7.

FOOD FOR THOUGHT...

1. Why do you think God wrote the Bible?

   To help us grow in Him and to learn about all that He did, starting at Creation. —GENEVIEVE, AGE 12

2. What goal for Bible reading would you like to set/have you set for yourself?

   I am going to try to read a chapter of Proverbs each day. —ABBY, AGE 13

3. Name a story/person in the Bible who has had a positive influence on you/who you admire. Why?

   David inspires me to do things that would help me from my mistakes and be a better person through the toils that I go through every day. —ETHAN, AGE 15

4. Why do you think it would be good to form a habit of reading and applying the Bible daily, even as a kid?

When you enter adulthood you want to have the strongest relationship with God as possible so that the pressures of the world won't suck you in. So the earlier you start developing your relationship with God the stronger you will become as you get older. The semi sheltered life of an American kid is the ideal time to start that relationship with God. —ZACH, AGE 14

5. What do you think is the most important thing about Bible reading?

You get a better relationship with God and you get to know Him better. —BRIGHTLY, AGE 9

CHAPTER 2
Action & Adventure
THE UNDERDOG
JUDGES 6, 7

Abundle of wheat dropped to the ground and unraveled. There stood Gideon, face ashen with fear. If he thought that an invasion by the enemy army was going to be frightening, he certainly hadn't anticipated the possibility of an angel of the Lord appearing before him.

The angel sitting under the looming oak tree in the yard said, "The Lord is with you, Mighty Warrior." *Mighty warrior?* Gideon thought. Then, like so many of the other godly men in the Bible, he thought, *You've got the wrong guy.* He certainly didn't feel like the Lord was with his people, nor did he consider himself a mighty warrior. He considered himself more of an underdog; a weakling among his family. The Lord told him, however, that he was going to lead an army to conquer the Midianites (who were rivals with the Israelites). He assured skeptical Gideon that He would be with him. Being in such a state of shock, Gideon pleaded for a sign that the angel truly was the Lord's. Sure enough, after placing a piece of broth-drenched meat and some bread on a rock just like the angel commanded, the rock burst out in flames. After building an altar, Gideon knew that he was going to be in for a wild ride with all that God had in store for him.

God then told Gideon to destroy his dad's altar to Baal, a false god, as well as to chop down the Asherah pole (which honored the false god Asherah) next to it. Gideon obeyed; he did this at night, however, because he was scared. Once he'd broken down the tributes to the idols, Gideon then built the one true God an altar at the site. He couldn't admit it, but… Gideon felt kind of awkward…

"*It was Joash's son, Gideon!*" yelled an angry neighbor. Gideon slunk away from his window. It was the very next morning since he'd been out destroying the tributes to the false gods, and the townsmen outside were fuming about the broken altar and pole. Gideon listened attentively to the conversation as they spoke to his father at the door. "Joash, bring your son out here. He broke down your altar to Baal and your Asherah pole! *He must die!*"

"Nonsense," Joash rolled his eyes. "If Baal is a real god, then he can defend himself when someone breaks down his altar. Now, if anyone tries to fight for Baal, I'll see to it that they won't live to see tomorrow!" He looked at them sternly. Gideon quit hyperventilating and sank against the wall. *Obeying God's commands is not so easy*, Gideon thought.

Gideon began gathering an army to save his country. Although the army was coming together, he was still skeptical. He wanted without-a-doubt, rock-solid proof that God was truly going to use him to save his country. After all, what would be the point of a weakling rallying an army and failing? He cowered at the thought of being the punch line of every joke from Israel to Midian. Only God could bring any success out of this ordeal.

"Um, God?" Gideon whispered timidly. "I need a sign." Gideon was going to leave out a piece of wool in the yard overnight, and, in the morning, God was going to absolutely saturate the wool with morning dew, while leaving the ground completely dry.

The next morning, Gideon bolted out the front door and stepped in the droughty dust. The ground was dry, but what about the wool? Doubtfully, he made his way over to the location of the wool. He was almost afraid to check. He reached down and felt: wet! God was going to make him victorious! Now, this should have given him the absolute proof that he wanted. Yes, this certainly heartened Gideon, but he was still unsure! As thankful as he was, Gideon asked a second time, "Could I have just one more sign? Please?" In order to strengthen Gideon's faith, God graciously agreed to his proposition for a sign. It was going to be the reverse of the first sign: wet ground, dry fleece.

The first thing on Gideon's mind as he got up the next morning was the question of whether or not God had given him the awaited sign. He darted out his front door, once again, and unexpectedly splashed and slid into the muddy, dew-drenched grass. Cleaning himself off, he ran to the dry wool with not a molecule of water to be found on it. This sign was proof enough for Gideon—his convincing took no more. God was on his side, and he was ready for battle!

Gideon's newly founded army was camping by a spring when God told him some distressing information. "You have too many people." His statement was as plain and simple as that, but it sure came as a blow to Gideon. After all, he had mustered a good-sized army! After receiving instructions from God, Gideon followed through. "If any of you are scared, you may go." To his disturbance, twenty-two thousand men left. Staring blankly at the camp of ten thousand men remaining, Gideon had no choice but to put more trust in God.

God knew that there were still too many men in the army if He was truly going to show His glory to the country through Gideon. So He told him, "There are still too many. Take them down to the water to get a drink, and I will give you further instructions then." Gideon pressed his palm against his forehead and sighed, yet he trusted God and His promise. He led the small army down to the water, where they all scrambled for a spot to take a cool drink under the parching sun.

God informed him that anyone that was licking up the water like a dog was to go home. The rest of them, who were cupping their hands and bringing the water up to their mouths, were to stay. Gideon surveyed the thirsty volunteers. He sent home the ones lapping up the water, leaving only three hundred. Three hundred?! Gideon's miniature army prepared to invade their enemies nearby the Midianite campsite. The night before the invasion, God spoke to Gideon.

"Gideon, get ready, because it is time for you to attack the camp. I am going to deliver the Midianites into your hands. If you are feeling fearful, go down into the Midianites' camp and eavesdrop in. Trust me, you will be encouraged." Gideon was indeed feeling fearful, so down to the campsite he went, with his servant Purah at his side. He tiptoed through the densely packed mass of tents. Upon seeing a dim glow coming from one tent, he stopped and pressed his ear against the outside curtain.

"Listen to this dream I had," a man began as he told the dream to his friend. "A giant loaf of bread came rolling into our camp. It rammed into the tent, causing it to capsize and cave in!"

"Uh-oh," the other replied worriedly. "I'd watch out if I were you. The meaning of your dream is obvious—Gideon's army will defeat us, by the very hand of God!" Gideon leapt for joy and praised God as he confidently strode back to camp. He was ready to attack! Waking up his little army, he shouted, *"Get up! For the Lord has given you victory over the Midianite hordes!"* (Judges 7:15). He divided his army into three groups of one hundred, passing out trumpets and torches inside of empty jars as they split up.

The excitement and morale of his troops skyrocketed as he unfolded their daring game plan. "When my group gets here," he explained, pointing to a location he had drawn in the mud below, "we will blast our trumpets. And your group, stationed either here or here," he pointed to two other locations in his sketch, "will sound your trumpets at the same time, then shout, *'For the Lord and for Gideon'"* (Judges 7:18).

So their plans became actions. Everything went flawlessly. The Israelites doubled over with laughter when the Midianites ran out of their camp wailing in terror. As they pursued the fleeing enemy, the Israelites began rallying men from the different tribes of Israel—soon enough, Naphtali, Asher, the whole Manasseh, and Ephraim were on the Midianites' tails. Another victory for the Lord!

IDENTITY CRISIS

The weakling of the family was the one who defeated Israel's enemy! Gideon proves to us that God's view of us is the one that truly matters. As 1 Samuel 16:7 says, "…The Lord doesn't see things the way you see them. People judge by outward appearance, but the Lord looks at the heart." God saw Gideon as a mighty warrior, and sure enough, he lived up to that description! It didn't matter that he was from the weakest clan in the tribe of Manasseh, or that he was the least in his family (Judges 6:15). God had made up His mind when He chose Gideon as the leader of the miniature army.

Gideon seemed pretty self-conscious. It took a lot of convincing to get him to believe that God was actually going to use him, of all people, to conquer an enemy! If I had to guess, I'd say Gideon was finding his identity in what others thought and said about him. How did he know he was the weakest? Why did he think he was incapable of doing what God had for him to do? Somebody could have told him those things, or he could have deduced it by looking at himself through the eyes of man. So now, the question is… how do we see ourselves? Do we know who we really are? Who do we think we are? Who do people think we are? *Who are we?*

MADE IN HIS IMAGE

God knows your identity as a fact. He made you, so He obviously knows everything about you. Let's say you wrote a fictional book, and you invented every character in it. Every single like and dislike that your main character possessed, you made it. Every single struggle and trial your character faces, you know it. You know your character's personality, nature, and, well, everything about them! Any surprises, or unknown facts you find out about your character? No. Obviously not—you are the creator of your character.

Similarly, God created us, and He knows every inch of our lives. We didn't create ourselves. He did! So, we should take God's Word for it when He tells us who we are. I think that King David puts this idea particularly well in Psalm 139. I recommend you read the whole thing. He writes about how God understands every aspect of us, how He sees us wherever we are, and how He made us.

Who does God say we are, anyway? We are "fearfully and wonderfully made" (Psalm 139:14 NIV). God didn't make any mistakes on us—He made us wonderfully! In Genesis 1:26-27,31, we find out that God made us in His image: the model used for making humans was God Himself! Not only that, but after He made man and woman, He stepped back, took a look, and called His creations good! And that's just humans in general—wait 'til you hear what God says about His followers!

Read Galatians 3:26 to find out what is said about the children of God. *Children of God*—He calls all who have faith in Jesus His sons and daughters! As believers, we're all God's children (1 John 3:1).

We have been given the mind of Christ (1 Corinthians 2:16), which means we are smart! We are capable!

SAY WHAT?

So, now that we know that we are each a valuable and precious treasure in God's eyes, what do we do with other people's opinions of us? If their opinions align with God's opinion of us, then it is okay to believe that. Does their opinion build us up? Does it add anything positive to us? Is it lovingly truthful?

But, what about when someone says something destructive? Hurtful? Attacking our personality, appearance, or skills? Attacking our character? If it gets in one ear, let it go out the other. Just move on; don't let it get to you. The devil will try all he can to get you to believe lies. He'll send friends, family, and strangers, well-meaning and otherwise, to tell you that you're not worth as much as you really are: sometimes by a joke at your expense, sometimes by a thoughtless comment, or sometimes by a flat-out rude comment with the sole purpose of destroying your emotions. As Christians, we have God on our side, ready to help us battle whatever destructive thoughts or words come our way. One great weapon is the Bible—also known as the Sword of the Spirit (Ephesians 6:17)!

Believe God's words over the words of people. People are inevitably going to say things they don't (and do) mean that are hurtful because they are human. Never let your identity be found in earthly, human things or defined by humans, who all have a sinful nature. God will always speak one hundred percent truth and edification. Cling to your identity in Christ—what He says is all that counts. Don't let what others say affect you. If others are being hurtful towards you, let a trusted adult know. If you can, stand up to the attacker! You set them straight on the truth. Not only that, but make sure they know their worth and identity in Christ—they are just as priceless! Always know that as a believer, you are His!

Just as we all know that it is no fun to be put down, we need to make an effort to build others up and avoid all negativity. We can find something edifying to say about everyone if we try hard enough.

SWISS PRISONER ROBINSON
ACTS 27, 28:1-10

Picture this: a ship full of prisoners screaming like little girls. The ocean heaved up frothy waves and battered against the remains of their ship. The soldiers, too, screamed as if they were falling off a cliff. Monstrosities of cumulonimbus clouds blotted all light from the firmament. Cargo flew overboard and crashed into the angry, tempestuous waters below like a melon-sized boulder smashing through a glass window. The buffeting roar of the water sounded like a blasting canon. How did we get to this disastrous visual? Let's rewind.

Slrig elttil ekil gnimaercs srenosirp fo lluf pihs a....

"Where is this ship headed?" Julius, the gruff centurion, asked a sailor loading some grain onto a ship. Italy, he found out, was the grand destination.

"Great! Could these prisoners and I come along? We have lost many valuable days at sea because of these unpredictable winds." Julius frowned thoughtfully as he remembered the strange weather from the past few voyages. The sailor nodded and the ship set off shortly afterwards. The capricious winds, once again, began affecting the course. The captain stopped the ship at Fair Havens, where they pondered their next move in the fickle ocean.

Julius favored a certain prisoner on board named Paul. With sincere urgency, Paul warned the crew, "I can tell that we shouldn't go on this trip. If we do, we are taking too great a risk for our cargo and the lives aboard!" The captain proclaimed his words to be nonsense, and insisted that the boat leave the harbor as soon as possible. Julius waved off Paul's negative warning and took the captain's appealing advice to keep sailing. Mostly everyone agreed. So they departed the harbor in hopes of making it to Phoenix before winter. Paul shook his head; disaster was brewing quickly.

A soft breeze brushed along the misty sea, and puffs of white cloud raced against the sun.

"See, Paul?" Julius pointed out, "Smooth sailing. Look, you're a smart fellow when it comes to prison behavior, but please—don't tell me how to sail." The crew felt satisfied with the smooth sailing, and they continue along the shore of the island Crete. Yet, in a matter of hours, that "soft breeze" became an overwhelming hurricane wind—the dreaded northeaster. That ship flew around like a ping-pong ball between the ocean's paddles. Here's where we insert that first stormy visual!

The storm picked up the pace heavily. For days, the men continually tossed their cargo overboard, littering the ocean floor with their possessions. Barely anything remained within its boards. All hope seemed lost. However, Paul had an announcement from the Lord, so in his chains, he shouted over the noisy windstorm.

"Listen, everyone! See how horrible this storm has become! You should have listened to my advice to wait to sail!" Julius humbly nodded. *"But don't lose hope. The God whom I serve sent an angel to tell me that none of us will be destroyed. Only the—"* Crash! An icy blast of water collapsed on the deck above. *"Only the ship will be lost. God is gracious to spare our lives. He still wants me to have my trial before Caesar. Be courageous, men; I believe that what God says is true. Still, we need to find an island to land on!"*

On the fourteenth night, the sailors realized that the water in the Adriatic Sea was getting lower. The sailors, panicking and afraid for their lives, secretly tried to escape on the lifeboat. Paul panted to Julius and the soldiers, "Nobody's life will be saved if these men get away!" The soldiers quickly foiled the attempted escape by cutting the ropes to the lifeboat, leaving it to freefall into the cyclone below.

Paul begged the starving men, "Please! Eat something to survive! Don't worry about the storm. Not a hair on any one of your heads will be lost." Paul passed around a bread loaf, which was scarfed down rapidly by the skeletal men. All 276 men ate to their stomach's content, and the rest of the grain went overboard to free the ship of extra weight.

The next day... *"Land ho! Land ho!"* cried one sailor after spotting a distant shore. Just as they aimed the ship towards the land, it hit a sandbar—and crumbled to pieces. Now, the soldiers had planned on killing the prisoners in case of a shipwreck so that none of them escaped. Julius, however, stopped them from following through with this for Paul's sake. As a matter of life or death for the prisoners, he yelled, "Jump if you can swim! The rest of you, grab onto a plank or board!" Everyone made it to the sandy shore safely, drenched and chilled to the bone.

After everyone had shaken off and experienced the joy of being on land after two weeks of seasickness, they found some island natives and asked them what the name of the island was. Malta was its name, and the inhabitants were hospitable and kind. A light drizzle fell upon the chilly island, so the natives built a roaring fire for the new-comers. Paul collected some scattered brush to throw into the blaze. Tossing it in, he felt a sharp pinch. A viper had latched onto his hand! The islanders jumped up and gasped. They stared intently, expecting him to swell up, experience serious symptoms, or even drop dead.

He's probably a murderer, and Justice won't let him escape, they thought. Paul nonchalantly shook off the snake and made himself comfortable by the fire. Nothing happened. The shocked crowd gasped once again, changing their minds. *This man is a god,* they thought.

The natives' chief, Publius, lived close by. He invited everyone into his house and, for three days, entertained his guests with the utmost hospitality. Publius's father was in bed with feverish sickness. He was in a miserable state. Paul prayed and laid hands on him, and he was healed! The islanders were most hospitable and generous to those on the ship. Once it was time to sail again, they furnished the crew with anything they needed.

Fear is a Virtue

Paul has a pretty amazing story. Do you know anyone who's been a shipwrecked, viper-bite surviving prisoner? Neither do I. He went through a lot in his Christ-centered lifetime, yet he trusted in God at all times—even during the turbulent times. Paul wasn't a god, but it is evident that He had the one true God with him. His lifetime was truly an adventure story. Paul knew that to live in fear just wouldn't do; he had to hand over his whole trust and place it in God's hands. Can you imagine Paul, the "model Christian," being afraid all the time? He wouldn't have gotten anywhere! If you've read from the book of Acts, you know that his life wasn't "normal." He has a radical, awesome testimony of repentance, endurance, faith, and love for God.

Actually, come to think of it, Paul did live in fear! He lived with the fear of God. Fearing God doesn't mean that he thought God was scary. This type of fear is more of a reverence. We need to fear God (Psalm 96:4)! Of course, part of fearing God means that we dread His judgments and we fear to step outside of His commands. We need to be so conscious of the consequences to not walking with the Lord that we steer clear of sinning and we obey God. We definitely shouldn't think God Himself is scary. So, Paul led a life of reverent fear.

Fearing God is considering Him with honor. He is superior to us. This kind of fear is essential in our Christian lives. We need to know that He is the Boss, and that He is in charge. Plus, Proverbs 1:7 says, "Fear of the Lord is the foundation of true knowledge..."

I encourage you to look up more verses on the fear of the Lord. See what God's Word has to say about this kind of fear—not a phobia, but a respect and healthy "dread" of disobeying. Every Christian should fear God as their Master and revere Him as their Lord.

Paul, however, did not live in the being-scared kind of fear. Had he let being afraid of speaking in front of people keep him from doing so, he wouldn't have led near as many people to Christ and helped out as many churches in his ministry. Had he worried about being mocked, he wouldn't have written such forward, impacting letters. Had he feared being physically hurt and in danger, he wouldn't have had the guts to value his beliefs and the gospel more than putting himself at risk.

Fear Management

Now, it is perfectly natural to be afraid. In fact, some fears are healthy in moderation. For instance, being afraid of cliffs is, obviously, a healthy fear to have. That way, you won't put yourself in danger of falling. In fact, this example fear should probably fall into the common sense category. Yet, sometimes fears can become so extreme that they are dangerous.

How can a fear be dangerous?! Well, say you had to pick between facing your fears or denying Jesus. Depending on the fear, this example may sound a bit extreme. Or is it? If a fear is so tremendous that we would rather deny our faith in Jesus than have to face it, then it is unhealthy and needs to be uprooted. So, where's the danger? It endangers our soul. If we deny Jesus, then He will deny us (Luke 12:9).

Fear could be a hindrance if it keeps us from following through with God's will for us. What if Paul had let his fear of public speaking (1 Corinthians 2:1-5) keep him from sharing God's Word with the crowds? What if he had said, "Wow, God… you've given me all this insight on life and Scriptures, but I just can't share this with the Romans. You know I don't like speaking in front of people. In fact, I am mortified of public speaking. Sorry, God, can't do it. You'll have to find another guy." He wouldn't have been obedient to God or led anyone to Christ! Paul wasn't very good at public speaking (2 Corinthians 10:10), but that didn't keep him from doing it for Christ's sake. Though he was afraid, he had far too much fear of the Lord to let the fear of speaking stop him!

What are you afraid of? I can't stand spiders, heights, and tickling. These fears could be dangerous if I would rather avoid them than stand up for my beliefs. Yes, I know it sounds silly to think that I would ever be faced with a situation where I am forced to either deny my beliefs or face one of those fears. But seriously, test your fears. Would you rather face them and stay true to your faith? If the answer is no, then the fear is unhealthy and, let's face it—dangerous.

Satan's Socks

There seems to be a diagnostic phobia for everything these days. I think the funniest one is *hippopotomonstrosesquippedaliophobia*—

the fear of long words[1] (ironically). God doesn't intend for us as Christians to be afraid (excluding moderate healthy fears and the reverent fear of God). 2 Timothy 1:7 (NKJV) reads, "For God has not given us a spirit of fear, but of power and of love and of a sound mind." God hasn't given us any fear, so fear isn't from God! And, if fear is not from God, then who put it in us?

What if you had a whole box full of clean, spotless dishes after a laborious day of toiling over the sink (pretend your dishwasher was broken and you had to hand wash each one)? Then, someone walked in and threw an oil-dripping, mud-caked, deep fried, smelly, disgusting sock into the dish box. That would be totally out of place! A soiled sock does not go in a box of clean dishes. The spirit "of power and of love and of a sound mind" that God has given us is like a box of shiny dishes. Then, Satan walks in with a filthy sock, or fear, and tosses it in where it doesn't belong. Bleh. What is fear doing in our spirit?!

Sounds like time to re-wash those dishes. How do we rid our lives of fear? God has given us many remedies to fear, and it's high time we take advantage of them. A few of these remedies include Scripture memory and repetition, prayer, and counseling. If a fear begins to develop, or if one is already active, Scripture memorization and repetition is a great way to feed your mind and spirit what is right. It's vitamins for the mind and spirit! Search a Bible concordance for verses on fear and on courage. Some verses I would recommend are Psalm 23:4, Psalm 27:1, Psalm 27:3, Psalm 34:4, Romans 8:15, and 1 John 4:18. Practice and quote the verses when

---

1   "hippopotomonstrosesquippedaliophobia." *Dictionary.com*'s 21st Century Lexicon. Dictionary.com, LLC. 22 Nov. 2013. <Dictionary.com http://dictionary.reference.com/browse /hippopotomonstrosesquippedaliophobia>.

any fear arises and stand upon them firmly. Don't let yourself doubt them.

Another way to fight off fear is by prayer. Talk to God—tell Him the fears you struggle with. He knows what they are, and He wants to help you. Let Him walk you through scary times and restore your spirit. Pray specific verses, as mentioned above. God's Word never fails (Isaiah 40:8).

In any situation when we're struggling, it's always good to get some counseling. I don't necessarily mean professional counseling; I mean talking to a trusted adult. I talk to my parents, and they give me great insight and help me out on whatever issue I'm facing. Grab your parents (preferably), pastor, youth pastor, or other godly Christian adult in your life and pour out your heart to them. In all matters, it's good to have an adult around to confide in and keep us accountable.

Never let fear control you. You control fear—as Christians, we have God fighting on our side, so we don't need to fear our enemies. Fear is just another enemy, so don't give in!

Knowing our identity in Christ and fighting fear are two crucial strategies in our spiritual lives. We need to equip ourselves with the tools and weapons needed in order to face life in this fallen world. Life with God is so exciting, and, if Jesus is in your heart, you're along for the ride! As we unfold more and more of God's awesome Holy Bible, we discover that the Christian life is full of action—it is, without a doubt, an adventure.

I DARE YOU...

Anyone struggling with self-image? Memorize Psalm 139:14. Don't let the devil whisper lies to you about who you are, because he will try and then you will have to fight for your beliefs. Every time one of the enemy's lies sneaks into your mind, push it out and quickly declare the verse. Not only will it be a great reminder to practice your verse, but you will be attacking those lies with the truth. Don't just say the words, but believe them and mean them!

I'd strongly encourage you to memorize 2 Timothy 1:7, especially if you battle with fear. Every time you face something you are afraid of, let that be a good reminder to practice your verse. Again, don't just say the words, but believe them and mean them!

FOOD FOR THOUGHT...

1. What does it mean to "fear God?"

   It's not to be afraid of Him, but it's knowing Him in a deeper relationship in a more personal way. It's also respecting Him and honoring Him. —KAYLEEN, AGE 12

2. What are the benefits of fearing God?

   Living a better life. —BAXTER, AGE 11

3. What are you afraid of? Why?

   The devil. —ALLIE, AGE 9

4. In which ways do you find it easier to fight fear?

   I usually use Scripture verses because the Word of God actually overpowers the fear. —SAM, AGE 13

5. Name one way that Satan interferes with our identity in Christ.

   He tempts us into believing other stuff. —THOMAS, AGE 12

CHAPTER 3
Crime Thrillers

BETRAYED

MATTHEW 26:14-27:10

Notorious double agent Judas Iscariot, the conniving so-called follower of Jesus Christ, sold Jesus's life to his enemies for a purse full of money. Although his horrendous betrayal played into God's perfect plan to save the sinful human race, Judas's position as one of the twelve disciples, so close to the Son of God, makes his disgusting double-dealing with the hateful Pharisees and Sadducees all the more despicable.

The clinking of the thirty silver coins in the sack Judas clutched sounded of his evil success. The chief priests and the elders smiled to themselves after making what they felt was a "fair trade"—they paid Judas, a disciple-gone-wrong, to turn in Jesus, number one on their "wanted" list. Judas walked away, feeling accomplished with his wicked deed. He lived by a rule: anything for money.

During the Passover Feast, Jesus said to his twelve disciples, "One of you is going to betray me." Shock and dismay filled the room as each disciple feared that it might be himself. In horror and confusion, one of the disciples spoke up for the rest, pleading to know who would be guilty of such a gross sin. Each turned pale as he asked if it would be himself—no one wanted to be the traitor.

"*One of you who has just eaten from this bowl with me will betray me* (Matthew 26:23)." Finally, Judas Iscariot mumbled, "*Rabbi, am I the one?*" *And Jesus told him,* "*You have said it*" (Matthew 26:25). A gasp and an icy silence fell in the room.

"*Hurry and do what you're going to do* (John 13:27)," Jesus told Judas to the confusion of the rest.

Criminal guilt written all over his color-drained face, Judas slipped into the black darkness of the empty night streets in a hurry. The disciples exchanged bewildered looks amongst one another at the strange scene they had just witnessed.

The confusion did not last for too long; after dinner, Jesus and the remaining eleven disciples visited the garden of Gethsemane. Jesus prayed earnestly, knowing what lay ahead in the coming hours. As he spoke with His Father, Jesus knew what He had to do in order to save the world, and He was ready and willing—but in so great a state of distress that He literally sweat drops of blood in His agony. The disciples—they slept. Jesus came back to them several times only to find them sprawled across the grass, lounged over rocks, and snoozing against a tree trunk. Then, Jesus woke them as He saw a band of soldiers and people approaching.

"Get up! The man who betrays me is here."

The mob approached, and Judas appeared amongst the clubs, swords, and flaming torches. They had worked out that Judas would let them know which man was Jesus by kissing His cheek. So Judas moved forward with his wretched plan.

"Greetings, Rabbi!" He kissed Him, and the men grabbed Jesus to arrest Him. The disciples, who were by now wide-awake and horrified, were bursting at the seams with anger and terror. Peter lashed out with a sword and cut off the ear of the high priest's servant. The servant flung himself down on the ground with a scream of sheer pain, holding the side of his head where his ear had been. The outraged disciple panted as he prepared to wipe out the entire mob of his master's enemies with his weapon.

"*No! Put the sword away!*" said Jesus. Jesus?! Why was He telling him to put the sword away? Didn't He want to be spared from this cruel mob? The disciples stood numb with surprise. Jesus put His hand over the servant's ear and healed him. "Those who live by the sword will die by the sword. If I wanted to be saved this death, I could just call on my Father to send me armies of angels. But, if I did that, then the Scriptures could not be fulfilled." Then, he turned to speak to the mob. "Why do you come at me with your swords and clubs? You never tried to attack me when I preached to you daily in the temple. But this is your hour, as it was written before—when darkness reigns." Then the mob took Jesus for his trials—then, they crucified him.

So Judas had committed his crime—his name was from then on chained with his criminal record of betrayal. People across the globe recognize him as one of the worst bad guys of the Bible. After Jesus's death, Judas's guilt finally gripped him—he realized what he had done. His head spun as he raced to the temple. There he hurled his thirty pieces of silver down on the floor with all his might at the feet of the priests.

"I have sinned," he declared, *"for I have betrayed an innocent man..."* (Matthew 27:4).

"That's not our problem. You're the one to blame," was the abrasive reply of the priests.

Judas ran to a field and hung himself.

DOUBLE-CROSSERS AND EX-FRIENDS

Of course, the story of Jesus's crucifixion has a joyful ending—He resurrects three days later, resulting in the hope of eternal life for all those who believe in Jesus and invite Him to be the Ruler of their lives. On the other hand, Judas's story, sadly, did not end well. Judas, one of the worst traitors who ever lived, made a wretched decision that many infamous people throughout history have made: the decision to reject Jesus—the worst decision anyone could ever make.

What a terrible way for Jesus's crucifixion to come about—one of his twelve closest friends double-crossed him! Of course, Jesus knew from the start that Judas was never truly loyal. While we don't know betrayal or disloyalty to the extent Jesus knew it, we can probably relate in one way or another to feeling hurt by a friend. I can think of several instances where someone's thoughtless words or actions have hurt me. In times that we've been tricked or wounded by a friend's words or actions, we may feel like we're the only humans who've ever experienced such turmoil. The Bible encourages us by showing that many other godly people have had to face trials and hurts by friends—Jesus being one example. There's also Paul and Barnabas having a heated dispute over whether or not to take John Mark on their trip (Acts 15:36-41). Joseph hurt from betrayal by his own brothers when they ruthlessly sold him into slavery (Genesis 37:12-36). Job had major friend trouble with his three condemning friends doing anything but helping and encouraging him in his time of agony (pretty much the whole book of Job!).

Been There, Done That

Sure, our everyday friend encounters may not be as extreme as some of these examples, but we can learn how to analyze our own situations, the minor and the major, by observing those of the godly people who had encounters with disloyal friends. For instance, we can see that although Judas's wicked trade probably distressed Jesus, He knew that God's plans were for the good of all of mankind. No, He didn't look forward to the horrendous death ahead of Him, but Jesus put His full trust in His Beloved

Father—He never placed his trust in the hands of any human or any force, only the Father. As He is the perfect example, we too should love and place all of our trust in our Heavenly Father. When we hand over all of our sticky situations, friend issues, and hurts to Him, we have a one hundred percent guarantee of satisfying results—God's in control (Psalm 31:14, 19-20; Romans 8:28).

Joseph has a remarkable testimony of forgiveness. Obviously, the hatred of his brothers that he had to experience deeply wounded him, but he chose to dispose of his anger towards them and, instead, to love and forgive them. His story is another example about how "… God causes everything to work together for the good of those who love God and are called according to his purpose for them" (Romans 8:28). When we invite Jesus into our hearts to be the Ruler of our lives, we are inviting him to take over every aspect that makes us up—that includes our relationships. Let Him give and take away; cherish and take good care of what He gives you, and release what he takes away. However, we need to strive to protect healthy relationships (and inevitable ones—like family) in our lives. Bring problems and hurts before the Lord, and seek His never-failing counsel.

Job, under the pressure of his criticizing friends (plus barely enduring the added sorrow, pain, and rejection), chose not to believe the lies spoken by Eliphaz, Bildad, and Zophar. Instead, he set his eyes on the Most High. Yes, he despised himself during his time of ruin, but never did he once speak against God or curse Him (as his wife wrongly advised him to do). Remembering the truth, that he was righteous in the sight of God, Job could defend himself against his friends' remarks about his affliction coming about because of his sinfulness. He knew who he was, and he was not going to compromise the facts that he knew to be true with the nonsense his so-called buddies were attempting to fill him with. We need to know our identity in Christ and who we are—who Christ says we are—and never let anyone tell us differently about our confirmed facts.

Now, if you've been having friction with a friend or family member or someone, *please* don't compare them to Judas or Joseph's brothers. As humans, we all have faults and make mistakes in our relationships. Matthew 7:3-5 tells us to take care of the plank in our own eye before trying to pull out the speck in another person's eye. In other words, we need to fix our own problems before trying to fix someone else's problems. Friends and family are priceless gifts from God—not to be taken for granted, but we should guard our relationships from being hurt or broken off. We need to watch our actions to make sure we aren't being the cause of any pain to someone else. If we are the ones making a relationship hard, we need to go to the Word and see what God says about being a good friend. We should read up on the subject anyway, because it's always good to know what God says on all matters.

Good Friends

So, now that we've discussed many ways that people can be bad friends, what exactly does a good friend look like, and what is the good in having good friends? Proverbs 18:1 shows us that the unfriendly man is self-centered. So, good friends serve others. They don't mind going out of their way to help and spend time with others. Don't put it beyond a good friend to visit sick friends in the hospital, help out at a fundraiser for a buddy, or assist with the day's chores at a friend's house. We see in Proverbs 16:28 and

Proverbs 17:9 two things that separate close friends: gossip and dwelling on faults. Then good friends don't slander, and they forgive. They'll keep conversations kind, and they'll wipe the slate clean after a dispute. And, in Proverbs 22:24, befriending easily angered people is discouraged, for good reasons, of course. Good friends are patient—slow to anger.

What else? Proverbs 17:17 (NIV) tells that a good friend "… loves at all times…", and that a brother helps in times of trouble. In Proverbs 18:24 (NIV), we find that "One who has unreliable friends soon comes to ruin, but there is a friend who sticks closer than a brother,"—not to say that your own brother can't be that friend! So good friends are loyal. They won't leave you in the dust when trouble comes rolling in—they'll stick by your side. Then, Proverbs 27:6 gives credit to the "Wounds from a sincere friend…", which shows us that good friends will correct us for our own good when we're wrong. Going on to verse 9, we discover the secret to the pleasantness of a good friend—heartfelt counsel. Good friends give good advice. Don't be too surprised to hear wise advice from a good friend. And finally, Ecclesiastes 4:10 tells us that a good friend has our back—good friends help pick us up when we fall down.

Of course, there are more verses on friendship and relationships in the Bible. Search to see how many you can find. We should look to not only *have* friends with these characteristics, but to *be* good friends ourselves. In any relationship we are ever involved in, we should strive to apply these qualities to ourselves and to play our roles with godliness. Of course, as imperfect beings, we are going to make mistakes now and then, and so will those around us. However, we need to keep our eyes set on the prize—great, peaceful relationships. Press on towards the goal!

FIBBING PHILANTHROPISTS

ACTS 5:1-11

"Sold," declared Ananias with the joy of a successful realtor, "The property sold!" His wife, Sapphira, clapped her hands gleefully as she gazed upon the heap of money sitting in front of her husband.

"Look at all this money!" cried Sapphira as she sifted the cash with her hands. "What ever are we going to do with it? I'd love to buy myself some fancy clothes... and you've been needing a new donkey! Ananias, please tell me you weren't thinking of giving all this hard-earned money to those apostles and the church? Oh, how I'd love some silks..." She looked off wistfully, imagining her reformed wardrobe. Ananias nodded in approval, thinking of all the advantages to a new donkey.

"Of course not, Honey! I was thinking of keeping a portion for us, and giving them the rest. They don't have to know that we kept some. That'll stay between you and me. And, speaking of donkeys, I may swing by the market tomorrow to view the farmer's selection on my way back from dropping off the money with the apostle Peter..." For the rest of that evening, the couple proposed lavish and extravagant ideas about the ways they would spend their new money.

Knock, knock...

Ananias entered the house to find Peter and some of the church elders and members gathered around a table. Proudly setting his purse full of money on the table in front of Peter, With a puffed up chest full of pride at the thought of how good this act of bountiful generosity was going to look to the apostles and the church, Ananias said, "This was all the money we received from selling the property." Peter boldly looked at him straight in the eye with a glint of sadness lingering around in his eye. He slowly shook his head.

"Oh, Ananias," Peter scolded. "Why have you lied to the Holy Spirit and kept part of the money from your land for yourself? It was never wrong for you to keep some of the money—the land you sold was rightfully yours. The money you made off of it was also yours, and it was at your disposal. What, then, prompted you to lie about the sum? You haven't lied to men. You've lied to God." At this, Ananias froze in a blank gaze. He dropped face forward, dead. Peter and the other men wore grave, somber countenances.

Some younger men wrapped up his body, took him away, and buried him.

About three hours passed before oblivious Sapphira walked into the house. She greeted the men and inquired as to where her husband had gone. She had no idea of the dreadful event that had occurred just a few hours prior to her arrival.

Peter held up the purse full of money to Sapphira and looked at her soberly. "Tell me, Sapphira, was this all the money you and Ananias received from the property?"

Sapphira blinked blankly and, trying to sound as innocent as possible, responded, "Oh, yes! Every coin of our profits!"

"Why do you challenge the Spirit of God? The men who buried your husband are just outside; they'll bury you next." With that, she collapsed at Peter's feet, dead on the ground. The young men who had buried Ananias came in to find yet another person to bury, so they carried Sapphira's body out to bury next to her husband's. The church heard about this disturbing event, and terrible fear gripped their hearts.

Liar, Liar

We've all heard the term "little, white lie," referring to lies that appear to be harmless and somewhat innocent. Let's bust this myth once and for all: There is no such thing as a "little, white lie." Yes, some lies are more harmful than others: someone committing treason on their country through a network of lies will be more harmful than a student pulling the cliché "the dog ate my homework" excuse on the teacher. Nevertheless, sin is sin and lies are lies, no matter how big or little the lie may be or seem. And lies are a much bigger deal than they are usually made—do you know who's in charge of the lie department? Satan. He's the father of lies (John 8:44).

Ananias and Sapphira may have thought that they were telling a little, white lie to Peter when they claimed that they had given all the money they'd earned from their sold property. After all, they didn't want the church to be angry at them, so they figured they might just make the whole deal sound better—sugar coating the truth a little bit—that way, they could keep the peace and still have some money to enjoy. Right? *Wrong.* They had lied to God. Their offering wasn't what they said it was.

God considers lying such a serious matter that you can find it in the list of some of the most hated, abominable things in the Lord's eyes. In Proverbs 6:17, the Bible says that the Lord hates a lying tongue. It is *detestable* to him. Yikes. There is a lot of power in the words we say, and we will have to give a reason for every single little thing we ever say (Matthew 12:36; Romans 14:12)—good, bad, idle, true, false—which should give us all the more reason to be honest! God knows the truth, even if we don't tell Him, so we might as well save ourselves judgment by going ahead and being honest (Hebrews 4:13). It's to our advantage.

WORTHWHILE WHOPPERS?

Lying is never good, even when it appears like it may be helping. For instance, the Word specifically addresses a situation in which someone could possible justify lying. In Romans 3:7, Paul gives the scenario of someone asking why they are still sinning if their lie makes God's truthfulness sound better and by doing so, gives Him more glory.

It's not a dumb question; it's perfectly legitimate to wonder why it's wrong to lie "for the Kingdom of Heaven?" Take witnessing, for example: why can't someone giving the gospel message to an unsaved friend add on some things to make the case sound more convincing? Why can't they say, "When Jesus comes in to your life, He takes all your troubles away and shields you from ever having any more trouble in life?" It's not true, but it might make the argument sound better. The friend, after hearing this agreeable (yet false) piece of information, might be convinced because of that one point and then say, "Okay, I want to invite Jesus into my heart to be my Savior," with expectations that Jesus is going to make life a walk in the park. Then, when trouble comes after their salvation, they may fall away because they think "Jesus has failed them." So, lying to make the things of Christ sound "better" and "more appealing" can make for some serious issues. Paul explains this dilemma well in Romans 3:5-8.

As Christians, God is calling us to share the gospel and the good news of Jesus with others. If we build for ourselves a reputation of lying, then why would anybody want to believe what we have to say about this Christ and eternal life stuff? If we lie about everything else, then what would make someone believe us when we're telling the truth?

JUST LYING

You may have played the fun game *Two Truths and a Lie* to get to know a group before. The name is pretty much self-explanatory, and it's a great icebreaker. I tell you two truths about myself and one lie, and the group casts their votes on which one they think is the lie. The best way to make it hard is to not make the lie sound crazy—for instance, I could make my lie: *I used to live in a cave on the side of a mountain.* Well, chances are, I probably didn't live in a cave on the side of a mountain, so everyone is probably going to vote for that one as the lie, and get it right. Or, I could make my lie sound possible. Here are my three statements—guess which one is the lie! *I like raisins. I've been bitten by a monkey. I have four sisters.*

Did you cast your vote yet? My lie was the first statement: *I like raisins.* I do not like raisins (sorry, Sun-Maid), but it sounded like it could have been a truth. The monkey statement sounded a bit more far-fetched, yet that one was true (take a petting zoo monkey's word for it if she doesn't want to be held).

So, where am I going with all of this? There is a difference between joking and lying. In this game, we realize that some lies sound an awful lot like the truth. Have you ever heard someone say one of these "lies in disguise," then vindicate it by laughing and saying, "Just kidding!" A joke sounds like a joke. Anyone can tell it's not true. A lie is not always easily figured out to be false. If someone tells me there's a T-Rex behind me, I'm going to laugh and automatically know there's not a T-Rex behind me; that's obvious. Anybody can tell that that's a joke. But, if someone tells me there's a big wolf spider behind me, I'm going to scream and run and panic. I'm not going to think it's funny (I'm not a big spider enthusiast... at all)! The person may laugh and say, "It was a joke!" but no, no— it was a lie. Another difference between jokes and lies: jokes tend to be funny and, most of the time, harmless. Lies, on the flip side, are pretty much just destructive.

Proverbs 26:18-19 gives a great analogy on this type of false joking: "Just as damaging as a madman shooting a deadly weapon is someone who lies to a friend and then says, "I was only joking." Wow. The example itself sounds bad. A madman shooting a deadly weapon! That's enough to keep anyone from pulling any of these joke-lies. I'm all for a good friendly joke, but when joking becomes lying, it's time to rethink our sense of humor.

The Father has commanded us to live according to the truth (2 John 1:4). There is so much more on truth, honesty, and lying in the Bible that I couldn't possibly fit it all in this short little section. Although telling the truth is not always easy (in fact, many times it is hard), honesty is an essential quality in the life of a believer. I would encourage you to read up on the subject in the Bible. The Bible is truth (John 17:17)! Every word within is true. From how the earth was created to who God is, every word in God's Holy Book can be trusted. If we are going to be imitators of Jesus, as we should be (1 Corinthians 11:1), we will be truthful, as Jesus was. Jesus is the truth (John 14:6)!

We've seen and learned from the criminal acts of some bad guys in the Bible. There are so many more criminals to be found in the Bible, and so much to learn from the mistakes of others. We can look at a situation from the standpoint of the victims in a situation (as we did with Judas's betrayal of Jesus) to learn how to respond to a crisis, or we can look from the standpoint of the guilty ones (as we did with Ananias and Sapphira's lie) to investigate what they did wrong and learn from their sinful actions so that we don't repeat them. Either way, God gave us the Word for us to learn about many things, including righteousness. Don't forget that

Christianity is not a religion or a list of do's and don'ts, but rather a relationship. If we love God, we'll obey His commands—therefore, we seek to follow him and pursue righteousness. Walk closely to God, and continue to dive into the Word, unwrapping all of God's loving letters to us!

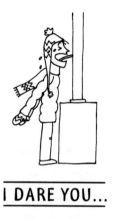

I DARE YOU...

Do you have any friends that have been, well, *not* friendly lately? Pray for them. Extend kindness to them. Is it easy? No, it can actually be quite hard sometimes. Do you have a sibling or cousin who hasn't been treating you all that well? Join the club, we've all been in a sticky relationship situation. What are we ever supposed to do about it? Pray for them. Extend kindness to them. Sometimes, treating your family with respect can be harder that treating your friends with respect. Find a special way to show them kindness, despite their actions. Write them a letter or note. Offer to help them clean their room. Scoop them some of their favorite ice cream (okay, you can scoop yourself some, too). Matthew 7:12 wraps up this concept well: "Do to others whatever you would like them to do to you. This is the essence of all that is taught in the law and the prophets."

Lies lead to lots of trouble in life. Ask a trusted Christian adult in your life to tell you about a time when a lie caused them a lot of unnecessary difficulty. Ask them why they regret the situation and what they think would have gone differently, had the truth been told. Or, ask a godly, Christian friend, sibling, or adult to keep you accountable about the things you say. Give them permission to point out to you every time you tell a half-truth or a lie, or even times when you look suspicious enough to have lied. Let them encourage you to go back and tell the truth, however tough that may be. Be teachable, and soon, lying won't be such a natural thing to do.

FOOD FOR THOUGHT...

1. Can you think of any other examples in the Bible where someone had trouble with a relationship(s)?

   Thomas, because he would not believe in Jesus unless he could put his fingers through his wrist and put his hand through his side after he rose from the dead. —RYLER, AGE 11

2. What does it feel like to be betrayed/hurt in a relationship?

   You feel like you've wasted time. You thought you knew the person and you've dedicated so much to them that it's not a good feeling for them to turn and slap you in the back like that. —BENJAMIN, AGE 14

3.   In what ways can you personally be a good friend?

You should be loyal, truthful, and kind. —LYDIA, AGE 11

4.   When is it hard to tell the truth?

I think it's hard to tell the truth when you think someone might judge you, or you're afraid of getting in trouble. —KRISTI, AGE 16

5.   As a believer, why is it important to be honest?

So we can show others that they can trust us. How could they tell that you were telling the truth about God's forgiveness if you weren't honest in all areas of your life? —JEREMIAH, AGE 14

CHAPTER 4
Love

MOTHER-IN-LOVE

THE BOOK OF RUTH

For the last time, get the donkeys ready!" Elimelech ordered his son, Mahlon. "You and Kilion should have packed when I told you. Now, let me find your mother." Elimelech alerted his wife, Naomi, that it was high time their family hit the road to Moab. In search of his brother, Mahlon went inside their empty house, where Kilion loitered before the big move.

"Time to go," Mahlon informed Kilion, "The donkeys are saddled up, and father is ready to hit the road." With a nod, Kilion followed his brother outside. After what seemed like ages to their father, the family was finally exiting Bethlehem, Judah. After all, a famine was no time to stick around.

The family planned to be gone a while; what they didn't plan on was that none of the men would be returning. They settled down in Moab, and tragedy struck: Elimelech died. Naomi and her sons grieved the loss of the man of the family. It wasn't long before both boys married women from Moab: Orpah and Ruth. The loss of their father was definitely hard, but at least now something joyful was happening in their family.

Yet, once more did disaster strike. The family now consisted of three widows. The two sons died just ten years after arriving in Moab, leaving their wives heartbroken and widowed. The three lonesome women mourned their devastating loss. Naomi, after hearing that God had ended the famine, decided to return to Judah. Shortly into the trip, she halted and turned to the girls.

"I can't let you come back to my country with me," she said. "Go home, remarry, and God bless you both for your kindness to my family." Both insisted upon going back to Judah with their desolate mother-in-law, but Naomi stood fast on her ground and vetoed their pleas. With tears, Orpah reluctantly parted after a heart-breaking farewell. Ruth, however, was determined to stay. She wouldn't budge; she held on to Naomi relentlessly. Between sobs, Naomi pointed to Orpah down the road back to Moab and choked out, "Go back to your life, your people, your gods!"

"No! I'm staying with you. *Wherever you go, I will go; wherever you live, I will live. Your people will be my people, and your God will be my God. Wherever you die, I will die, and there I will be buried. May the Lord punish me severely if I allow anything but death to separate us!*" (Ruth 1:16-17). At this, Naomi felt the true love that Ruth had for her. She couldn't turn her down.

"Is that—that's Naomi! Elimelech's wife! Everyone, look! Naomi's back!" cried a woman upon seeing Naomi coming through the market. Then, scrunching her face into a sour expression at the sight of her foreigner companion, she added, "And she's brought a Moabitess."

"Well, if it isn't Naomi! It's been forever! How've you been?" another squawked.

Eyes darkly sagging, Naomi looked at them with her glum expression and said, "Naomi, Naomi... enough! Don't call me that! God has brought misery upon me. I don't fit the name Naomi anymore. Call me Mara instead; a name meaning 'bitter' suits me far better." Naomi left without another word, leaving her audience to ponder her sudden emotional meltdown. Ruth followed alongside.

The next morning before sunrise, Ruth set to go to the fields. Hugging her mother-in-law tightly, Ruth whispered, "I'll be back before dark." She set off. Finding a nice field with several women already gleaning (or picking up the leftover grain that the harvesters dropped on the ground), Ruth joined in, loading the grain into her shawl. She toiled for several hours under the blazing sun.

Around noon, the sun was beating down on the field, and a drop of sweat maneuvered its way down Ruth's face, yet she continued her task. Just then, the owner of the field arrived from business in Bethlehem. With a contagiously energetic smile spread across his face, the master walked out to the field and shouted, "*The Lord be with you!*" to his harvesters (Ruth 2:4).

With a chorus of lively greetings, they responded with, "*The Lord bless you* (Ruth 2:4)!*"

The owner, Boaz, went to stand over by the field supervisor. In a low voice, he leaned over and, discreetly pointing to Ruth, asked him, "Who's that woman over there?"

"That," the supervisor began, "is Naomi's widowed daughter-in-law from Moab. She's been gleaning with the other women non-stop since early this morning, taking only one quick break." Impressed, Boaz walked across the field to talk to the girl.

"Excuse me," Boaz approached Ruth, who was speechless that the owner of the field was talking to her. "Hello! Welcome to my field. Please don't go away to another. You'll be safe here." He paused, and smiled. "If you get thirsty, my men have large jars of water filled up by the well. You can get a drink there."

Ruth, shocked by his hospitality, bowed to him. She begged to know why he would even bother talking to a Moabite like herself. He went on to elaborate on how much he admired her well-known generosity to Naomi, and Ruth bubbled with elation at being esteemed highly by the owner. Boaz invited Ruth to have lunch with him and the harvesters in the shade. After taking her fill of roasted grain, she had leftovers to bring home. After her refreshing lunch, Ruth got back to her diligent working. Boaz secretly ordered his men to purposely drop some bundles of grain for her.

Ruth gleaned away until evening. At the end of the work day, she bundled up all of her grain to discover that she had gathered a whole lot. She and Naomi delighted over the heap. After hearing that Ruth had gleaned at Boaz's field, Naomi lit up, and joyfully gasped.

"Boaz! He's a relative of Elimelech's. Oh, I'm so glad you found his field! Keep going there; you'll be protected there." So Ruth did, and Boaz continued to favor her greatly. Naomi, aware of the fact, brought up a startling proposition to her daughter-in-law one day.

"Ruth, dear, I cannot let you go on being alone. I want you to be happy—to have a safe home where you are loved and cared for. Boaz is a close relative, and he's certainly a great man of God, and, well, it'd be great if you could…"

Now, we all know where this is heading. Yes, Naomi was suggesting that Boaz would make a great husband for Ruth. She gave instructions about how to go about making a proposal. "I will do whatever you say," Ruth obediently responded. She proposed to Boaz, following all of Naomi's steps. Back in their day, proposals differed greatly from modern day proposals, as you can probably tell. Carrying out Jewish tradition, Ruth slept at Boaz's feet until he awoke.

Boaz, although honored and pleased by her proposal, discovered a flaw in the plan: "There's a relative nearer than I," Boaz responded, stroking his beard as he was deep in thought. Back then, the nearest relative got first pick on inheriting the widow and land of the deceased; that is, if he accepted the offer. But Boaz assured Ruth that he would do all he could to inherit her himself. Before she left, he gave her some grain to take home. Ruth hauled her overflowing shawl back to Naomi. She smiled to know that Boaz was in favor of their marrying, but then, the thought of the closer kinsman stranger accepting the offer diluted her smile.

After explaining the dilemma to Naomi, her mother-in-law guaranteed her that "…The man won't rest until he has settled things today" (Ruth 3:18). Ruth hugged her and showed her the shawl full of grain that she'd left at the door. The day wasted away with frantic nail biting and intervals of tedium as the women waited to hear from Boaz.

The door flung open a sharp 180 degrees on its hinges. "Ruth!" cried Boaz in elation as he burst into Naomi's house. "We're going to be married!" Surprise and joy were heavy in the atmosphere, and everyone praised the Lord.

"I nearly lost Elimelech's property, along with Ruth," Boaz told them as he pulled his beard thoughtfully, as he recollecting the legal meeting. Then he smiled and said, "Of course, once my cousin heard that marrying was part of the deal, he hastily allowed me to have the inheritance. His money is his priority."

It wasn't long before they married. They had a little boy named Obed. Obed grew up, got a wife, and had a son, as well: little baby Jesse. In a few decades, Naomi's great grandson Jesse got married and had kids of his own! Seven sons, actually: Eliab, Abinadab, Shammah,… these may not sound familiar just yet. His youngest son, however, is the famous one. Jesse was the father of little shepherd boy David, who grew up to be a skilled warrior and the godly king of Israel, as well as an ancestor of the Son of God: Jesus Christ.

LOVE IS CALLING

God gives everyone purpose and callings. Have you ever wondered what He has called you to do or what purpose you're here to fulfill? You may be thinking, *Well, I'm too young to do mission work in the South American jungles or something like that. What kind of calling is there that a kid can do?* Well, first, everyone's calling is personal. God might call Kyle to be a pastor, while He calls Jane to be a teacher. Second, you're never too young to be fulfilling your callings! Sure, you may need to wait until your adulthood before flying to the South American jungle to witness to natives there (if God calls you too), but you have plenty of other callings that beg for fulfilling now. What callings, you ask? The *calling to love. God* has called everyone to love.

It's no surprise that love is our calling, because the word *love* pretty much wraps up everything we're supposed to do. We'll obey God's commands if we love Him. We'll go to South America (at the Lord's command) if we love Him. And if we love Him, we'll love others. The examples are endless! Now, God knows that we won't always love Him like we're supposed to. In fact, it's bound to happen, because we're humans, not God—He is the only one who can love perfectly. Just know that, when we fail to love Him as we should, God is always here to pick us up and give us another chance. His greatest commandment is to love Him with everything we've got, so we should strive to obey it (Matthew 22:36-37).

God called Ruth to take care of her hurting mother-in-law and to marry Boaz, which was part of His plan in creating Jesus's genealogy. God's will is perfect, so there's no need to doubt that

He knows what He's doing. Even in difficult times, God is working together a perfect plan. He times everything perfectly, and He's got everything in control. Our callings are all a part of God's will.

God has also called us to obey our parents, do our schoolwork, invest in our family and friend relationships, and keep up with our responsibilities. The "little things" count in the Kingdom of Heaven. Jesus even said that when we faithfully complete the few little tasks that God entrusts us with, He will then open more doors and entrust us with more of His heavenly missions and duties (Matthew 25:21).

I remember the first day my mom let me put a plug in the electrical outlet by myself. I felt so grown up as I proudly plugged in my kid-sized sewing machine. Then, in a couple years, I could plug in outlets *and* answer the telephone all by myself. Then, give a few more years, my parents let me plug in outlets and answer the telephone *and* play in our neighborhood without an adult—and the responsibilities and privileges continue to stack up! I was faithful with not having any accidents with the outlet, so they added an extra privilege. I was faithful with answering the telephone politely and asking permission before calling people, so I got another privilege. I was faithful to abide by the rules and boundaries of our outdoor escapades, so my parents gave me more entrustments. See how it works? Just like my earthly parents, God is a good parent, and when He sees that we are faithful with one task, He will give us more, because He knows we are becoming even more responsible and trustworthy.

Yes, when we help out by scrubbing the dishes, giving our little sibling a hoist to reach the soap next to the sink, and collecting the portfolio full of papers Dad just spilled, we are pleasing God. Why would He care? Well, first of all, God is the Father of all people who've invited Jesus into their hearts; therefore, like any good father would, He cares about every aspect of our lives. Secondly, when we do the little things with a cheerful attitude and to the best of our ability, they aren't so little anymore—they fall into the love category (I told you that love wasn't all mushy). If we love God, we'll obey His callings for us, no matter how big or little they are.

You don't have to try hard to come up with not-so-little things to do to show love in everyday life. Ask your dad to teach you how to play that game he loved as a kid. Ask your mom what her favorite dessert is and if you can help her bake it this weekend. Does your sister need help with her math worksheet? Fix your brother a snack after he comes in from mowing the lawn. Does your friend's family need any help unpacking boxes at their new house? Hold the door open for the elderly couple slowly walking into the restaurant. And that's just one category of Love—caring.

Unrequited Love

Loving, however, is not always as easy as showing those not-so-little acts of kindness. Sometimes loving is hard. It's okay—Jesus didn't guarantee that loving would be easy or fun. He did, however, guarantee that we can do everything through Christ who gives us strength (Philippians 4:13). So, with this unfailing strength force on our side, we can love like Jesus does. And when we make mistakes, we have Christ's strength on our side to get up off the ground, dust ourselves off, and try again, continually aiming to love unfailingly.

Christ's strength is the power that helps us withstand the bad weather in life. Sometimes people take the love we show for granted, and sometimes our acts of kindness don't seem to be recognized or appreciated. Thankfully, we aren't stranded on this island alone—Jesus has been through those sort of frustrating situations. Read Luke 17:11-19 to find out how Jesus mercifully cleanses ten lepers from their disease, and receives only one thank you—from a Samaritan, a hated neighbor of the Jews!

We shouldn't love and expect something in return. God sees our every move, and He is also fully aware of the acts of love we show, even when not a single person can testify to it. He is pleased and smiles down upon us, and rewards us, because we are storing up treasure in heaven, rather than hogging earthly possessions for ourselves (Matthew 6:20). So love without expecting payment, and then be rewarded by the Lord, who gives better gifts than any human ever could (Matthew 7:11).

A veteran in selfless loving, Ruth knew how it felt to be treated wrongly while loving. The Jews weren't fans of the Moabites, and she got a taste of their incivility. Yet, keeping her priorities straight, she chose to pour out her daughterly love on her helpless mother-in-law, instead of running back to Moab crying because she was despised for her ethnicity. Love always perseveres (1 Corinthians 13:7).

Our loving progress doesn't affect God's love for us—His love for us will always be the same: perfect, unfailing, unfathomable, incomparable, *huge*... the list of adjectives goes on and on. But, just like any good parent, our Heavenly Father is overjoyed when we make accomplishments. He's there, calling, "That's my kid!" when we show love with a joyful attitude.

The Bible is all about Him who is Love. By reading the Bible, we get a better idea of what love really is. Love is sacrifice; love is forgiveness; love changes lives. Read 1 Corinthians 13 for a high-definition image of true love. It's so much more than paper hearts with *Pixy Stixs*.

THE ARROWS ARE BEYOND YOU

1 SAMUEL 20 NKJV

"The arrows are beyond you? Oh Lord, no—please no!" David shook in his distress. Panting heavily, he put his hand on his forehead as his mind whirled round and round. Jonathan ran around the large stone, and David bowed down three times as the tears trickled down his sorrowed face. Jonathan squeezed him and began sobbing into his shoulder.

"David," he shut his eyes tightly as tears spurted out, "I'm so sorry." David managed a slight smile to encourage his beloved friend, yet the agony in him weighed down. Jonathan's father, King Saul, had been overtaken with jealousy when David was receiving so much attention as the future king of Israel. Now Saul sought his life. Both David and Jonathan felt excessively mortified. David sought consolation by praying and writing psalms to the Lord, who continued to carry him through that frightening time. Jonathan, grieved that his own father could be such a wretch towards his best friend, offered his services to David and helped him flee for his life.

For quite obvious reasons, David planned to be absent from a holiday dinner at the king's house. Jonathan had worked out a code to warn David, who'd been taking refuge in the fields, of his father's true intentions. "The arrows are on this side of you," would mean that the king behaved coolly once notified of David's absence and that all should be safe. "The arrows are beyond you," on the other hand, would give David reason to fear for his life—Saul was furious!

The moment of truth arrived. Saul noticed that Jonathan arrived to the holiday dinner without his best friend by his side. Not taking his narrowed eyes off of his son, Saul slowly made his way over to his rightful place at the table. Jonathan squirmed; his heart began to beat faster.

"H—Happy New Moon Feast, Dad," Jonathan squeaked out nervously. Suspicious, Saul inquired as to where David was.

"He's... not here." *Wham!* Saul slammed his fist on the table. Everyone jumped.

"*I can see that he's not here!*" With his burning anger in hot flames, Saul launched a fierce argument, whirling his rage at Jonathan. In misery, Jonathan cried, "Why should he be put to death? What has he done?" Gritting his teeth violently, Saul flung his spear at Jonathan—and missed. His son flew out of the room in a heat of anger, prepared to warn David at the break of the following dawn.

Shooting an arrow nearby the rock David hid around, Jonathan sent a young servant boy to fetch it. As the boy sprinted across the field, Jonathan called out, "The arrows are beyond you!" In other words, "Danger! Father is *mad*! Run for your life!" After the oblivious servant boy fetched the arrows, Jonathan sent him back to town, trying to look as composed as possible. The two friends wept in agony together. Jonathan, despite his father, was loyally by David's side—even in his friend's darkest hours.

No Greater Love

"There is no greater love than to lay down one's life for one's friends" (John 15:13). This verse shows us the greatest form of love—sacrifice. We see it all over the Bible—Ruth sacrificed the life she was used to in order to be a comfort to her mother-in-law. Jonathan gave up his own security and favor in his evil father's eyes in order to save his best friend's life. David knew what loving was all about—and he didn't even have to read Paul's love chapter (1 Corinthians 13—which, by the way, was written hundreds of years after David's lifetime) to know it!

David, God's choice for Israel's new king, the husband of Saul's daughter, Michal, and best friends with the king's son, Jonathan, loved even Saul himself—the king that sought to take his life. No, that doesn't mean that David aimed to be best buddies with the king, but it means that he still honored, respected, and recognized Saul as God's appointed authority, despite the king's cruelty. In fact, even after the king's death, David regarded Saul with the highest respect as God's anointed one (1 Samuel 24:10; 2 Samuel 1:14). It's not that he particularly liked Saul as a friend or admired anything about his character, but he loved him as God did.

Of course, we can't forget Jonathan—giving up any honor his father would have had toward him for turning in the number one on his wanted list because of his devout brotherly love for David, who was more of a brother than a friend. He put his life in danger in order to save David's life. Nothing but death could separate him from his best friend. He, for sure, is the model friend!

When we sacrificially lay down our lives, we humble ourselves and regard others as better than us. We are following Jesus's example. The sinless Son of God laid down His life for us, the ultimate act of love!

SACRIFICING THE COOKIE

It's not instinctive human nature to consider others better than us, so we have to make a clearly conscious effort—I mean, if I'm getting a cookie off the tray, my first inclination will be to pick the biggest, most chocolatey one, and not think of anybody but me, myself, and I. I need to be aware that maybe there are other people in this house besides me, myself, and I who'd like the biggest, most chocolatey cookie. This, of course, is a minor crisis in which I will probably succeed in picking the right answer—let my sisters have the first pick. But what about when showing love by sacrifice really counts—and it doesn't just affect my chocolate-craving taste buds? Conveniently, I know a Book that equips us with all the sacrifice-skills we'll ever need to show love to others—can you take a wild guess at which book I mean?

Pretty much all love is sacrifice. If we are patient, as love is, then we are giving up the opportunity to go with those impulsive angry feelings that cause us to itch up on the inside. If we are not rude, as love isn't, then we miss the moment where we could've made someone laugh with a clever, funny insult about our friend who isn't here. If we don't keep a record of wrongs, like love doesn't, then we lose great comebacks to fire at an accusing opponent. Sometimes sacrificial love isn't just giving up an advantage, but it's giving up the instinctive desire to go with the sinful human nature in every one of us.

So, we have to sacrifice getting ourselves the greatest advantage (the biggest cookie) or the option that feels best (yelling in anger), and go out of our way to treat others like we want to be treated? *Ugh! That sounds like work.* Yes, it is work, but it pays well! Imagine the blessings and benefits we'll reap from regarding others better than us and sacrificing our little (and big) luxuries. We'll obtain favor not only in the eyes of others, but in the eyes of God (which is most important). Besides that and many other benefits, we'll feel good. There's a distinct kind of pleasure that comes from making others the priority. Still unsure if all this sacrificial love is worth it? Try it! You'll like it.

At the end of the day, we all have to face the fact that nobody but Jesus is perfect. Therefore, if we aren't perfect, we won't love perfectly—and God knows that. We need to desire to be perfect like the Father (Matthew 5:48), and make the best effort to love everyone with brotherly, godly love. Loving God is, of course, the first step to living a life of love. Then, show love in your family— love does start in the home, after all. Show love to everyone—that was Jesus's lifestyle.

The Creator of Love wrote the Bible—an act of love in itself—in order to guide us in loving. He did it because He loves us far too much to let us miss out on having a relationship with Him and eternal life by His side. God tells us about all of love's traits so we can apply them, because, like stated earlier, love is the ultimate goal—it wraps up all of God's laws (Galatians 5:14). In order to love, we need to have a model to compare ourselves with. Jesus, the Son of God, is the perfect model of perfect love.

I DARE YOU...

Spontaneously give a gift to a brother or sister. If you don't have any siblings, give a gift to a cousin or friend. This is about the time when the popular phrase, "I'm broke," gets used. The most mean- ingful gifts don't always cost money (Don't believe me? I'll name five: time, effort, counsel, praise, encouragement). Or, you could give something you already own or something handmade—keep the receiver in mind: thoughtfulness is all about targeting what that specific person likes or enjoys (For instance, don't buy your sister a milkshake if she's lactose intolerant, don't offer to play checkers with cousin Timmy if he is outspokenly against all forms of board games, etc. You know how it goes).

Or, depending on your age, consider taking your sibling out for ice cream, pizza, etc. Can't drive? Whip up something creative at home. Whatever you give, whether it be purchased or homemade, edible or inedible, material or immaterial… even if it's simply the gift of your time, let your sibling know your love for him/her (don't panic—this may not look like breaking all ice and saying, "I love you, Freddy," to your brother, it may just be a matter of getting the message across in other ways—ways to make it obvious to Freddy that you do, in fact, have sincere brotherly love for him). It's not awkward, it's what God expects of us as His bondservants. It may *feel* awkward at first, especially if you're new to the idea, but feelings should not determine our commitment to follow God's orders. Besides, this is a dare.

FOOD FOR THOUGHT…

1. What does love mean to you?

It means to praise, to encourage, to sacrifice, and to share the hope of Christ. —TOMMY, AGE 11

2. What are some specific callings that God has in your life right now?

   Family. —ALIVIA, AGE 10

3. Name someone who has been a great example of love to you.

   My mom, because she's caring and thoughtful. —ASHLIN, AGE 13

4. When is it hard for you to show love?

   It's hard to show love to someone when they don't show love to you. —JP, AGE 11

5. Name some ways to show love to your family.

   Through humility, love, and to be a servant. —JEDIDIAH, AGE 14

LOVE

Thy hair is as a flock of goats

Song of Solomon 4:1 KJV

CHAPTER 5
Poetry

THE WRITE RESPONSE

BASED ON PSALM 3, 2 SAMUEL 15:13-37

King David's heart felt heavier than a cart full of rocks as he ached with sorrow under the light of the dim candle flicker that lit his dark tent. He dipped the tip of the quill into the ink and poured out his troubles to God:

O Lord, how many are my foes!
How many rise up against me!
Many are saying of me,
"God will not deliver him."

Tears fell from his eyes as he hid his forlorn expression in his palms. He mourned over his son, Absalom: a rebellious delinquent who had just declared himself king over Hebron, and was now prepared to hunt down his father. He had the whole city turned against his father. David was familiar with running for his life, but...from his own son?!

Now, more than ever, David needed his Father by his side.

But you, Lord, are a shield around me;
my glory, the One who lifts my head high.
I call out to the Lord,
and he answers me from his holy mountain.

Even in those simple lines he had just penned, David felt a slight sense of comfort enter him. He remembered that God was still the same God, no matter what circumstances, and that the Lord would guard him, encourage him, and give him the answers he needed.

David began feeling vitalized as he hastily scribbled down the new inspired lines for his poem.

> *I lie down and sleep;*
> *I wake again, because the Lord sustains me.*
> *I will not fear though tens of thousands*
> *assail me on every side.*

God was giving King David the stamina to endure these trying times. The tens of thousands were, indeed, assailing David from all sides, yet the agony would have remained just the same had it been only his son. He was, however, empowered by the encouragement that the Lord was in control. David sighed with relief at the thought that *he* wasn't the one in control. Feeling the weight of the sinfulness on earth, David groaned in his sea of painful emotions and anguish, and he placed his plea in God's presence:

> *Arise, Lord!*
> *Deliver me, my God!*
> *Strike all my enemies on the jaw;*
> *break the teeth of the wicked.*

David was tired of enemies. They were always tracking him down and attacking from every corner. He was going to leave revenge in God's lot; God could punish his enemies better than David could, even if he had the fiercest army. King David closed his eyes and took a deep breath. He felt at peace after laying down his cares at His loving Father's feet. He ended the psalm on an empowering note:

From the Lord comes deliverance.
May your blessing be on your people.

TRUST AND OBEY

After all that King David had to go through in his lifetime, why didn't he just give up? Why didn't he just stop caring about life and do whatever he wanted? David held a key to happiness, hope, and endurance. David had his hope in the Lord, the only One worth putting hope in, and therefore, he had the strength to keep doing God's will. David's heart for the Lord can be seen throughout the majority of the book of Psalms. His full hope and joy is found in the Lord. David wrote in Psalm 20:7 (NIV), "Some trust in chariots and some in horses, but we trust in the name of the Lord our God."

People may fail us, but God never does. In any situation, He's in control. He's got everything coordinated according to His perfect plan. People ask, "So, why do bad things happen if God's in control?" Remember that good things can come out of bad situations. For instance, from a traffic-jamming car wreck God can remind Jordan how valuable life is, and to not waste the time that God has given him on earth. God might allow Kelley's family to experience tough financial times in order to teach them to be thankful for what He provides. Or, God might let the power go out so that Wyatt is left with no choice but to put down the video game control glued to his hands and spend a little quality time with his family. But sometimes, bad things happen, and we just can't find anything good in the situation. Even in bad times God can bring glory to His Name. When bad things happen, we can learn to trust in God.

When we invite Jesus into our lives, we are basically saying, "Okay, Lord. I'm surrendering everything to you. This isn't my life anymore—it's Yours. You're in charge now." Everyone has good and bad days, weeks, months, and years. If you've ever been in a bad situation, you know how exhausting it can be to try to juggle everything life's throwing at you. God wants us to stop—and just hand everything to Him. David did that. You probably realized that he didn't march right over to Hebron and ground Absalom for the rest of his life—which brings up another point. When humans are in control, it isn't all "smooth sailing." People don't have the power to do everything themselves. If people try to take care of bad situations by themselves without any help from God, they are just going to make a bigger mess.

May His Force Be With You

"…If God is for us, who can ever be against us?" Romans 8:31 tells us that, with God on our side, we have a guaranteed win—we have the best force! He is always there for us. In life, we have to face a bunch of cliffs and decide how we will cross them. God will carry you through. "Just trust in me," He says. "People may laugh at you and call you weak for not trying to jump across, but that's okay. I'm on your side." Put your hope in the Lord, and you will be amazed at all you can accomplish with Him on your side.

During those times when there seems to be nothing good in a situation (for example, loss of a family member/friend, loss of a job, loss of an ability, sickness, etc), tell God about your feelings. He's there for you to share your heart, emotions, thoughts, and dreams. Don't vent anger or disrespect your Heavenly Father, but find comfort in His Word and through the hope that He gives us. Praise Him for whatever good you can find to give thanks for—even if it's simply the fact that He is in control, or that He loves you. We don't always need to understand why, but we do need to understand that when the God that created the universe with a few words is in control of our lives, we have no need to fear—who can ever stand against us?

SOLOMON SAYS

BASED ON PROVERBS 25, 1 KINGS 3:5-28

Have you heard of David's son, King Solomon? There was a time when everyone knew his name—he was famous! Renowned author of parts of Proverbs, possibly Ecclesiastes, and the Song of Solomon (also called Song of Songs), this guy was smart. Very smart.

Solomon paused to think up a good analogy for the profound proverb that had come to mind. God had offered him anything that his heart desired. What do you think Solomon chose? No, not to possess the strongest army or to be the richest man on earth, but he asked God for wisdom! Thrilled that he had asked for something so righteous, God granted Solomon's request. Not only that, but He lavished wealth and esteem upon him. Solomon was a blessed guy.

> Don't demand an audience with the king
> or push for a place among the great.
> It's better to wait for an invitation to the head table
> than to be sent away in public disgrace. (vs. 6-7)

Solomon figured that his example ought to be able to get his point across. He shuddered as he envisioned such an embarrass-ing scene: *A man walked into a party at the king's palace. Thinking so highly of himself, he gave himself a lofty seat near the head of the high table. Quite pleased to be showing off near the other men of high rank, he began an elaborate conversation with a well-admired official. As he was talking, the king came up behind him and tapped him on the shoulder.*

"Excuse me, sir. I'm afraid I must ask you to sit over at this other table," the king said, pointing to the other side of the great room, where all the people of little or no rank sat. The man got up from his seat with all eyes in the room glued to his cherry-red face.

Solomon nodded as he carefully wrote down this wise bit of insight that the Lord had placed in his mind. As most writers do, he needed a change in scenery. Getting up, Solomon walked to his window and inhaled a large whiff of afternoon breeze. He tried to brainstorm some possible examples for his next proverb. He went and sat down by the fire. The wood crackled and popped, and the coals blazed beneath the warm flames. Coals! A great analogy popped into his mind. Once again, Solomon had found a way to get his point across. Plopping back down into his chair, Solomon wrote down one of his most golden proverbs yet:

> *If your enemies are hungry, give them food to eat.*
> *If they are thirsty, give them water to drink.*
> *You will heap burning coals of shame on their heads,*
> *and the Lord will reward you.* (vs. 21-22)

His point was very simple: be kind to your enemies and serve them. They will feel convicted, and the Lord will reward you. Solomon's wise sayings occur again in the New Testament. In Romans 12:17-20, the apostle Paul writes to the Romans about letting God pay others back for their evil, rather than they themselves getting revenge. Little did Solomon know that people would be referring to his wisdom not only during his time, but even thousands of years later.

He continued writing more sayings as the Lord led until he felt that he had written all he could for the time being. His last proverb read:

> *A person without self-control*
> *is like a city with broken-down walls.* (vs. 28)

A city's walls are its protection. Without its protection, the city is open for any force to come and take it captive or to even destroy it. It works the same way with a person. Someone who doesn't have self-control has no protection to keep away forces that may try to take captive or even destroy that individual. Solomon knew that this was one of the most important proverbs he had written yet. As he rolled up the scroll he had been writing on, Solomon couldn't help but feel that he was blessed. He recalled one of his old sayings, Proverbs 3:13:

Joyful is the person who finds wisdom,
the one who gains understanding.

WISE MAN VS. WISE GUY

The English language is strange—a slim chance and a fat chance mean the exact same thing, while a wise man and a wise guy mean the opposite. Wise men are actually wise, and wise guys are, well, not. Throughout the book of Proverbs, the subjects of wisdom and foolishness come up frequently. In fact, the second verse in the whole book of Proverbs tells us that Solomon's proverbs serve the very purpose of obtaining wisdom. Wisdom is important, as we can tell. There wouldn't be a whole book in the Bible for it if it wasn't! Not only do we find wisdom spoken of in Proverbs, but the book of Job, Ecclesiastes, Isaiah, Jeremiah, Ezekiel, Daniel, not to mention Matthew, Mark, Luke, and Paul's letters, all make multiple references to it.

Why is being wise so important? Proverbs 4:6 tells us that wisdom protects and guards over us. In other words, wisdom is a safeguard that can keep us from a lot of trouble in life. It is so easy to get wisdom—James 1:5 (NIV1984) says, "If you need wisdom, ask our generous God, and he will give it to you. He will not rebuke you for asking." All we have to do is *ask!* Verse six goes on to say, "But when you ask him, be sure that your faith is in God alone..." Just ask with faith, and wisdom is yours!

I could not even begin to cover all the benefits of wisdom; "Wisdom will save you from evil people..." (Proverbs 2:12); "Joyful is the person who finds wisdom, the one who gains understanding. For wisdom is more profitable than silver, and her wages are better than gold," (Proverbs 3:13-14); "...wisdom is far more valuable than rubies. Nothing you desire can compare with it," (Proverbs 8:11); "If you become wise, you will be the one to benefit..." (Proverbs 9:12); and, "A man will be commended according to his wisdom..." (Proverbs 12:8 NKJV). Hands down, we need wisdom!

Proverbs tells us all we need to know about being wise, but it also tells us how to be foolish: "...fools despise wisdom and discipline," (Proverbs 1:7); "...fools hate knowledge..." (Proverbs 1:22); "... Fools are destroyed by their own complacency," (Proverbs 1:32); "...a foolish child brings grief to a mother," (Proverbs 10:1); "...the babbling of a fool invites disaster," (Proverbs 10:14); "...fools are destroyed by their lack of common sense," (Proverbs 10:21); "Doing wrong is fun for a fool..." (Proverbs 10:23); "...The fool will be a servant to the wise," (Proverbs 11:29); "Fools think their own way is right..." (Proverbs 12:15).

Wow. There is a pretty big contrast between wisdom and foolishness. Wise men know what is right, and they aren't too proud to take advice (Proverbs 12:15). Wise *guys*, on the other hand, think and pretend they know what is right, while they really aren't.

SANDCASTLES

Jesus gives us a parable about the wise builder and the foolish builder. The wise man decided to build his house on a solid rock. He finished it just in time to take shelter from a typhoon sweeping on to land. Although the waves battered it and the winds whipped against it, the house stood firm. Then, a foolish man decided to build his house on the sand. He finished just in time to take shelter from another typhoon coming through. Again, the waves battered it and the winds whipped against it, but the house could not stand against the storm, so it collapsed with a *crash!*

In this parable, Jesus was comparing those who listen and practice what He says to a wise man who is grounded in solid faith. He was also comparing those who listen but do not apply what He says to a foolish man who does not have a firm foundation in his beliefs. The wise man knew what was right, and he lived it out by building his house where he knew it was safe. The foolish man was a wise guy—he thought he knew what was right, so he decided to live that out by building his house on the sand. That didn't end too well for him, did it?

WHAT'S ON YOUR WISH LIST?

God appeared to King Solomon in a dream, and He said, "What do you want? Ask, and I will give it to you!" (1 Kings 3:5) and Solomon asked for wisdom! Sure enough, he became one of the wisest men to ever live. However, this brings up a good point—just because you have wisdom doesn't mean you automatically use it.

Being wise is a decision. We can see Solomon in his wisdom and his foolishness. Solomon ended up becoming famous because of his great wisdom, and the Queen of Sheba heard about him. She came over to try his wisdom by testing it with tough questions. She talked and talked about everything she had on her mind, but she couldn't stump Solomon! He answered every one of her questions with ease. She was astounded. She admitted to doubting the rumors she had heard of him, but every doubt was put to rest after her visit. She praised God after seeing the wisdom He had bestowed on his servant, Solomon.

Then, we see Solomon in his weaker, wisdom-forsaken moments. Solomon married women from different countries who worshipped false gods. He didn't just marry one or two... he married seven *hundred*. That is crazy—not to mention, foolish! I mean, can you name seven hundred friends off the top of your head? I know I can't! Not only did he pretty much "collect" wives, but he also "collected" horses, silver, and gold. Three things that the Lord had forbidden for a king of Israel: having multiple wives, stockpiling horses, and getting too rich (Deuteronomy 17:16-17)—Solomon managed to break those three requirements. If I had to guess, I'd say Solomon wasn't using his wisdom. Wouldn't you agree?

Solomon could have saved himself (and Israel) a lot of trouble just by exercising his wisdom. His foolish decisions led to Israel's division into two separate kingdoms. It's always more convenient to learn from the mistakes of others...so what are you going to draw from Solomon's mistake? Will you use your wisdom and make your life a thousand times easier? We can still learn from Solomon's wisdom, because when he chose to be wise, he was *wise!*

Feed your wisdom through the Book of Proverbs, the words of Jesus, and the writings of the New Testament writers.

———————————————————

Poetry can be a lot more than "roses are red, violets are blue." If you hear the back-stories to David's psalms, you can sympathize (or empathize) with him. When you stop and ponder Solomon's proverbs, we find that we can truly relate to nearly every one of them from a daily experience. Did you know that there are thirty-one quick-read chapters in Proverbs, just like there are generally thirty-one days in a month. If you're new to this idea of daily Bible time, reading a Proverbs chapter each day is a simple suggestion to get you in the habit. Every book and passage in the Bible is there for a reason. Even Deuteronomy, Numbers, and Ezra. Why do you think God put Psalms and Proverbs in His Holy Book? Every time you open His Word, God wants to talk to you. Actually, He wants to talk to you *all the time!* So don't keep your Heavenly Father waiting—talk to Him!

I DARE YOU...

Establish a new way of talking to God. Maybe you don't consistently talk with God, and today would be the perfect day to start. Go ahead, just talk to Him! He's your Friend, Father, Healer, Provider, King, Lord, and Savior! He wants to tell you amazing things. Starting and ending a day with prayer is an effective way to remember and form a habit of conversing with the Lord. What about when you're taking a walk? Riding your bike (scooter, skate board, Ripstik, roller blades, roller skates, etc.)? Fishing? Cleaning your room? Maybe you'd like to try a new approach to prayer. The possibilities are endless! Here are several ideas you could try:

1. Start a prayer journal
2. Buddy up with a close, godly friend and be partners in prayer
3. Sing praises to the Lord (yes, David was being literal—not metaphoric—when he spoke of singing!)
4. Pick prayer targets (some examples: every time you see a cemetery, thank the Lord for yet another day of life, pray for those who have lost loved ones, and pray that you would count

every moment as valuable for Jesus; every time you watch a thunderstorm, thank the Lord for the beauty of His Creation, marvel at His power and greatness, and pray for protection over the homes in your city)

Obtain wisdom. Pick the Proverb of the day (Is today the 23rd? Read Proverbs 23), grab a highlighter, a pen, sticky notes, a Bible encyclopedia, a Bible theology book, a seminary text book, an original copy of Webster's Dictionary, some band-aids in case of paper cuts, some... just kidding. But I do recommend those first three items as regular Bible-studying, spirit-food eating utensils (more suggestions in chapter 11). Ask a godly, trusted, Christian adult (preferably one or both of your parents) to give you their thoughts, biblical wisdom, and insight on a specific proverb. Discuss the truths presented and the practical ways that you can apply and live out those truths.

FOOD FOR THOUGHT...

1. What does it feel like to lay out your troubles before the Lord in prayer, as David did when he was distressed?

    When I tell God my troubles it feels like submission. It feels like I submit to Him. I humble myself to God and His plan.
    —MATTHEW, AGE 15

2. When is it hard for you to put your full trust in God?

   When nobody else around me does, or when it feels like there's no hope. —PEYTON, AGE 13

3. Name a time when God gave you something that you asked Him for.

   I prayed for a baby sister that looks like me. —KAYTLIN, AGE 8

4. Name some ways wisdom can benefit you.

   It can help you obey God and your parents, and it will make you a better person over all. —MADISON, AGE 13

5. Who has been a great example of wisdom to you? Why?

   My dad, because he reads the Bible everyday and knows answers to all my questions. —LUKE, AGE 7

CHAPTER 6

Science Non-Fiction

JURASSIC JOB

BASED ON JOB 40:15-24, JOB 41, ISAIAH 27:1

Listen to me, Job," thundered God. Pulling back some cedar trees, He pointed at a colossal dinosaur-like creature dropping its long neck down towards the ground to tear up a mouthful of grass for lunch. As it lifted its head from his feast and lumbered on to another nearby patch of green grass, God spoke.

"Look, Job," He said, "See how I made the behemoth so massive and powerful, yet it eats grass like a cow, and it lives in the hills, resting by the marsh. Look at its strong build! Its bones and muscles are sturdy; its tail swishes like one of these cedar trees. This colossal beast is secure and able to withstand the raging waters. Surely, no one but I, its Creator, can defeat it or take it captive. Such a docile, breathtaking animal!"

Job stared, awestruck, beholding the magnificent, yet intimidating, sight of the behemoth. Slowly clomping from grass patch to grass patch, the dinosaur was a living, breathing example of God's wonder. God then set back the trees and moved some vines aside, revealing a different creature.

"Job, witness the leviathan—a creature so fierce and mighty that no other can compare with it." Job looked out upon a vast, sparkling sea, but he couldn't see anything. Suddenly, a monstrous beast shot up from beneath the soft waves, creating an ear-splitting crash among the waters. The dinosaur hissed and spit flames and sparks as it exhaled, causing the air to fill with the dense smoke jetting from its nostrils.

"Here it is: invincible, fearsome, dangerous—yet graceful. Look at it glide through the water! Look at that wake of foaming water that trails behind after it disturbs the calm of the water! I made it firm; see that coat of spikes and shields armoring its back. Look at how I designed its mouth. Have you ever seen so many teeth in one place?" The leviathan let out a long, burning blast of fire from its mouth, giving Job ample opportunity to study the teeth, which had kept many a human from trying to mess with the beast. Fear filled Job as he locked eyes with the dragon-like lizard.

God continued, "See its glowing eyes, its flaming breath! It has tough skin and a hefty neck. Do you see those jagged scales I gave its stomach? You can only imagine the battering it gives anyone who tries to take it down. Hooks, harpoons, lances, clubs, spears, ropes, cords, arrows, darts, javelins, iron, bronze, sling stones… it's no use. The leviathan laughs at those who think that they can defeat it. It treats weapons like pieces of straw." Job shivered as the beast coiled up and writhed violently on the muddy shore, leaving jagged imprints from its stomach in the muck.

"Would you dare try to overtake this merciless beast? Would you dare try to disturb it? Would you try to make an alliance or a deal with it? Would you try to make it your house pet? Would you give your servants a leviathan on a leash to play with? No, of course not. It is menacing just to look at. How much more to try to defeat Me, the Creator of the leviathan!"

Paleontology, Anyone?

I think dinosaurs are so cool. It might not be so cool to encounter one, but they are incredible creatures to study. So many theories exist on dinosaurs—one scientist will say they did exist, another will say they didn't, some will say that they still do, and so on. Who do we believe? It's awfully hard to know.

I was reading the chapter in Job on the behemoth. I was imagining this massive, towering dinosaur swishing its cedar-like tail and marveling at this amazing creation, when all of a sudden, my interest dwindled as the little footnote down at the bottom of the page caught my eye, indicating that perhaps the behemoth was just a hippopotamus or elephant. What?!

The same thing happened with the leviathan. After imaging this colossal, fierce dinosaur and its fearlessness, I read the footnote, suggesting that perhaps this beast was merely a crocodile. It even said that the behemoth's tail that sways like a cedar may, in fact, be its trunk (which really doesn't make much logical sense, when you think about it). *Well, that's a disappointment,* I thought.

While researching a little bit about the leviathan, I came across an article on both of the dinosaurs starring in Job, and it clarified the misinformation in the frustrating footnotes. Not only that, but the article gave some astonishing facts on recent dinosaur sightings. I encourage you to check it out. In fact, the whole website is great for all things Creation! Visit the Creationist website *Answers in Genesis.* See the recommendations at the back of this book for information on where to find the article. Needless to say, my interest on the dinosaurs of Job was rekindled.

Strange that someone could make such a broad interpretation of such a clear image that the Lord painted for us about dinosaurs. Strange that someone could think that we evolved from monkey-humans rather than a Creator intelligently designing the human race, as clearly told in Genesis 1-2. Strange that someone could think that God used evolution to create the world and its inhabitants. We need to believe the Bible, word-for-word. Genesis 2:4 says, "This is the account of the creation of the heavens and the earth. When the Lord God *made* the earth and the heavens..." (italics mine). It said He made the earth, not that a "big bang" mysteriously occur and create everything. Genesis 2:7 says, "the Lord God formed the man from the dust of the ground. He breathed the breath of life into the man's nostrils, and the man became a living person." I didn't hear anything about a piece of goo climbing out of a swamp and eventually turning into a human, did you? God *formed* man! That's clear enough.

That's Yesterday's Translation

Throughout our entire lives, we will encounter people who, just like we've been discussing, will misinterpret or interpret text too liberally. These people will take the Bible, the law, the American Constitution, or any other important documents and say, "Well, this was written such a long time ago! It's terribly outdated, and not relevant to today's modern society. But if we switch a couple words here... flip a few words here... take out this whole paragraph... there! It fits!" Lots of times, these people simply want to make the text say what they want to hear. When Jesus is not the center of a person's life, evil can grab a hold and take root in that person's empty, godless heart. That's why we need to be grounded by the roots in what we believe, so that we can hold on to what is true and right in accordance with the Word, because there really are people out there inventing new ways of sinning (Romans 1:30).

The Word of God stands forever—people are not supposed to change it. Psalm 119:89 says, "Your eternal word, O Lord, stands firm in heaven." Did you hear the psalmist say, "Your word, O Lord, is eternal, until the 1960's, then it will probably be outdated, and it will need to be revised and modernized?" Me neither. Then, Isaiah 40:8 says, "The grass withers and the flowers fade, but the word of our God stands forever." The Bible is acknowledging that, hey, things get outdated! Things get old, and pass on and away— but the Word doesn't. It remains alive forever. So why don't people take God for His Word?

Has someone ever told you to "be quiet for a minute" and you took the words literally in order to get your way? I've done that many times. I would stop, watch the clock until it turned to the next minute, and then continue with whatever it was I was supposed to stop doing. Or, perhaps you were in hasty need of some assistance, and whoever was going to help you said, "Give me a second," and sure enough, you give them precisely one second before continuing to push and nag for help. I have also done that. We were obviously not taking those words in context. Believe it or not, there are people—even adults—today who similarly, take the Bible and throw it out of context to fit their cause or situation. There are some people that even want to attribute the process of evolution to God, saying that, since He can do anything, He could have used evolution to create the world. Yes, He could have, but

He didn't, as we read in Genesis 2:4-7. This belief that God used evolution is called theistic evolution, and it does not take God for His Word. Here's something you need to know: God never makes mistakes. Not in His Word, not in His Creation, not on anything. The Bible is true. God, my friends, never lies.

The Absolute Truth

"...the Word became human and made his home among us. He was full of unfailing love and faithfulness..." John 1:14 tells us that the Word became human—it came alive in the form of a human, God's son, Jesus! If you could put all of the Bible into a human, that was Jesus. Jesus is God in the flesh. The Word must be perfect, flawless, and true if Jesus is the Word in flesh! Jesus always told the truth. Did you know that the NLT Bible shows Jesus saying, "I tell you the truth..." sixty-eight times? That's a lot of truth! Jesus tells us in John 5:24, "I tell you the truth, those who listen to my message and believe in God who sent me have eternal life. They will never be condemned for their sins, but they have already passed from death into life." There it is again, "I tell you the truth!" Later, when Jesus prays in the garden before His death, He tells His Father, "Make them holy by your truth; teach them your word, which is truth" (John 17:17). Truth is a big deal to God! Don't you think He would go through the trouble to make sure that those who contributed to His Holy Book wrote one hundred percent truth in their passages? He did.

The problem with disbelieving the Bible on any aspect, such as Creation versus evolution, is that if you don't believe God on one thing, what's to say that you won't believe God on another? If you don't believe God on everything He says, how can you be confident in the things you do believe to be true? You can see how not believing God can cause some hard conflicts with belief. Believe God and His Word. If you believe *in* God, you will believe His Words. He says He made you and formed you. *Believe Him.* He says He loves you. *Believe Him.* He says that He will never leave or forsake you—*so believe Him!* If we lean toward either believing extreme, whether we never believe anyone or whether we always believe everyone, serious problems can arrive in life. It's good to know that we don't have to be cautious and filter anything that God says: we can completely, whole-heartedly, whole-mindedly believe everything He and His Holy Word say.

DIARY OF THE NEARLY DIGESTED

BASED ON THE BOOK OF JONAH

This afternoon, while silently praying during my walk along the loading docks, the Lord spoke to me. He told me to go to Nineveh and give the people a message from the Lord against their evil! I hope He was joking, because I will not go to the capital of Assyria to get killed! I have heard of their notorious reputation for ruthless cruelty, and I do not want to be the next public example. Besides, if I get slaughtered, how will I do the Lord's will?

Jonah

Today, I took my daily prayer walk through Aram's gardens. I spoke to the Lord about Nineveh, clearly letting Him know that my job as a prophet does not include throwing myself in harm's way. He told me, however, that I was going to go to Nineveh and preach to the people His message. Now I am fearful that the Lord will punish me greatly if I don't go, so I came up with a plan. I cut my prayer walk short, and I ran over to the loading dock to talk to Jakin. He and his crew sail to Joppa tomorrow morning, and I have arranged to go with them. Then, I will board a ship to Tarshish. The Lord will not be able to find me if I sail hundreds of miles in the opposite direction of where He usually finds me! I must get ready for the journey.

Jonah

I am aboard the ship to Tarshish. The sail from home to Joppa was smooth and peaceful. I think I stayed up too late last night, because I am terribly tired. I will probably go down below deck to take a nap in a few minutes. The food aboard is not so bad, but I didn't have much of an appetite to eat with that one idol with the owl-like eyes staring at me from the corner. They did bring quite a few of their idols with them on this trip. They arranged them all in corner on the deck. I can barely keep my eyes open. I need to rest.

Jonah

A lot has happened since my last entry earlier today. I am not on the ship anymore. I am… inside a digestive tract. Yes, you read correctly, a digestive tract. Let me back up a bit. The captain came and abruptly woke me up from my nice nap to tell me that we were about to die because of a tremendous tempest. I always knew I was a hard sleeper, but this was ridiculous. The captain called me up to pray to my God, because none of their gods were answering their pleas. I felt kind of awkward being asked to pray to the God that I was trying to run away from.

Up on deck, the men were bowing and begging the idols in the corner to save their lives. After a decision to cast lots to find out who was bringing bad luck upon the ship, the lot fell upon me, and I was forced to answer their interrogations towards me. "Who are you?" "Where do you come from?" "Why are you the cause of this storm?" They hurled questions at me from every side. I told them that I was a Hebrew who was running away from the God of Israel, whom I worshipped. God had sent the storm because of my sin. It was my fault that their lives were in danger, so I told them to throw me overboard. They, however, were so hesitant to throw me over, so they tried to row the ship back to land. Yet, the storm raged on harder, making it impossible to even try rowing.

Without another option, the men said a prayer to the Lord, begging for His mercy on them as they threw an innocent man into the ocean. Innocent man... yeah, right. Do you know the feeling of being hurled into the ocean, knowing that you're probably living your last hour? Well, I do. As I sank deep, I looked up and saw that the crashing waves above had ceased, and the surface of the water looked clear and fluorescently blue, as if the sun were shining through. I began to swim towards the light, when suddenly, I felt something cramming me in some tight, squishy, dark, smelly place from behind. There were all sorts of weird noises. I couldn't see the sunlight anymore. I lost sight of the surface of the water as well. I was ankle-deep in muck as I sat squashed between two squishy things. Carcasses of dead fish, soggy seaweed, and bits of fishing net lay all around me.

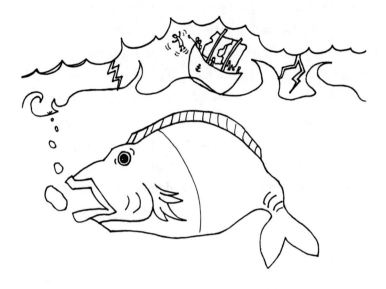

Suddenly, it occurred to me: I was inside a fish's body. I was never an expert fisherman, but this was no small fish. Who knows what kind of fish it was, but it was huge and hungry. I spent the next four hours marveling at the fact that I was not dead, but saved in the most peculiar way. Here I am now, wondering what will happen to me. This is probably my last journal entry, because I will probably die in a matter of minutes. I should be dead, after sinning so horribly against God. So there: I am inside a digestive tract.

Jonah

It has been a wild week for me. Inside of the fish, I did a lot of praying. I realize that being swallowed by a fish was not just some crazy, fickle turn of events, luck, or fate, but rather God's divine control over everything in His Creation. Although I should have died long ago for my disobedience, God is faithful, and He has a plan for me. After asking the Lord for forgiveness, I thanked Him for His merciful salvation. I was inside of that giant fish for three days and nights, but then, God performed yet another saving miracle. No, I did not die inside the digestive tract. Today, the fish was making some strange noises—stranger than the noises it made when I first got swallowed. Those squishy things inside of it were moving around in funny ways. Everything in the fish seemed to be churning round and round, when finally, in a split second, I found myself being vomited onto land. Land! Dry, solid land! Praise God! Once again, the Lord asked me to go to Nineveh and preach His Word. This time, I said yes. I begin my journey for Nineveh in a couple hours. It is amazing the measures God will take in order to accomplish His will. I will never try to run away from the Lord again. God sent a fish to swallow me this time, but who knows what He would send if I tried to run away from Him a second time?

Jonah

S.O.S.

I wonder how big the fish that swallowed Jonah actually was. Most of the children's story Bibles depict it as a whale, but the Bible never said that it was a whale! Nevertheless, God saved Jonah with that fish—even though he did not deserve it. Jonah was trying to run away from God (which, by the way, is an impossible task, so don't try it), because he was deliberately defying God's mandate to go to Nineveh. Remember, God is the perfect Father, so He gave Jonah grace, although He still issued a punishment (time out inside a fish) because of His great love for His son. God does the same for all of us. He is so merciful, and He saves.

God worked more that one saving miracle in the story of Jonah. Yes, he saved Jonah, but did you realize how the foreign sailors on the ship who were worshipping the idols at first then turned to God to beg for forgiveness? Well, that wasn't the end of it. Jonah 1:15-16 says, "Then the sailors picked Jonah up and threw him into the raging sea, and the storm stopped at once! The sailors were awestruck by the Lord's great power, and they offered him a sacrifice and vowed to serve him." Sounds to me like they began following the One, True God rather than their many idols! Not only that, but later, when Jonah goes to Nineveh, there is a surprising turn of events—the Ninevites repented, and God spared their city from destruction! Jonah was shocked... more so, he was angry. Very angry. But, that's a story for you to read on your own. Pull out your Bible and read the short yet intriguing book of Jonah!

He's the Boss

God is in control. He brings nations up and down. He controls the forces of nature. He gives and takes away life. He has designed every day of *your* life! Yes, God knows what you're having for lunch today, what the weather will be like this afternoon, and what's coming in the mail. He knows the thoughts you'll think, the emotions you'll feel, and the hurts and joys that will come your way. He is in control of the lives of believers and unbelievers.

When we invite Jesus into our lives, we are surrendering our entire lives to Him, and that means that He's the Boss of us. He calls the shots, we don't have a say in what happens. *Well, that sounds like no fun,* you might be thinking. Quite the contrary—life is so much better when God's in charge. We may think we know what's best for us, but God really knows what's best for us.

Take our friend Jonah for example: he thought it would be a great idea to tell God, "No, I won't obey you," and then run away from him. He thought he was saving his life from the death he expected from the evil Ninevites. Jonah obviously did not care about the fate of Nineveh, but God sure did. He said, "Oh no, you don't," and sent a big storm. After Jonah was submerging in the ocean, God reeled him in by sending a fish to swallow him up, giving Jonah a good, long chance to think about his actions and pray for forgiveness. Then, God gave Jonah a second chance by causing the fish to vomit him up onto shore. When you read the rest of the story, point out all the times that God provided or showed His authority in some way.

Get Out of the Driver's Seat!

So if God's way is so much better than ours, than why do so many Christians live like unbelievers? Haven't they surrendered their lives? If people don't surrender their lives to Christ, they are not putting their complete trust in God. They think that they know better, they can do it better, and everything will be better when they are in charge. Little do they know that things are the best when God is in charge.

A tourist is strolling through Time Square during his visit to New York City. He suddenly gets the inclination to see the city at its highest point: at the top of the Empire State Building. It's almost sunset, *he thinks*, I'd better hurry.

"*Taxi!*" *he calls. Immediately, a bright yellow taxi with a check-ered stripe on it zips up to his side. The tourist walks right up to the driver's side and opens the car door.*

"*Um, what are you doing?*" *asks the taxi driver with raised eyebrows.*

"*I need to get to the Empire State Building. So, if you wouldn't mind, please get out. I need to drive, and I want to make it there before sunset. I can't risk getting lost and losing time.*" *The tourist shoves past the bewildered driver who, by force, gets out of the car.*

"*Um, hello?! I am the driver! This is my job! I drive people around NYC day and night, every day! You think I would get lost on these roads?! Please—get out of the driver's seat!*"

Hmm… I wonder if we ever act like this control-hungry character. Are we reluctant to put trust in the "Driver" of our lives (not that we should trust every NYC taxi driver, but you get the analogy)? Do you think God, for His sake and ours, is asking us to, "Please—get out of the driver's seat?" This is an example of how it looks for those who won't give God their full life. They don't want to lose charge, because they think they can control their lives better than God can. Yeah, right! God isn't just an expert on life, as a taxi driver would be an expert on the streets of NYC, but He created life—He invented the whole concept! That's something I'm positive none of us have never done.

ANOTHER CHAPTER ON TRUST?

Trust God. He deserves it. Never place your trust in human power, because no human can compare to the Lord and His omnipotence (that's a good word to know: *omnipotent* means "infinite in power"[2]). He coordinates every move of Creation. I don't know about you, but I find that pretty amazing.

I know that we also talked about trusting God in the previous chapter, but this is such an important subject. I hope that you somehow have begun to see just how trustworthy, reliable, and faithful the Lord is. Many people, maybe even you, have been left not knowing who they can trust, because perhaps they have been hurt by someone they thought they could trust. If you get one thing out of this chapter, remember this: God's not like that. No matter what people tell you or what stories you hear, God will never fail you. He will never stop loving you with all His heart. He will never leave you or hurt you. He wants what is best for you. Hey, God made you, so why not trust Him with you?

I'd encourage you to look for some more "Science Non-Fiction" stories in the Bible! Ever read about a talking snake or donkey? What about a flood that wiped off the face of the earth? Some lions that just didn't feel like eating the man thrown into their living quarters? What about some birds that served as waiters and waitresses for a prophet in the wilderness? The Word of God is full of great stories for Sci-Fi enthusiasts, animal lovers, and science fans. The best creature stories come from the Creator Himself!

2 "omnipotent." *Dictionary.com Unabridged.* Random House, Inc. 22 Nov. 2013. <Dictionary.com http://dictionary.reference.com/browse/omnipotent>.

I DARE YOU...

Why do you believe what you believe? Who says that what you believe is truth? You may have always believed that stealing is wrong, but why is it wrong? Who says that it's wrong? Who are they to say that it is wrong? Pick a belief you feel strongly about (unfortunately, strong beliefs like "the Tigers are the best football team ever," and "I should be voted as president" are not valid answers in this particular dare), such as "stealing is wrong" and find at least three Bible verses supporting your claim. Don't forget the source of your claim—did Al Fergussen the high school know-it-all suggest it or did Jesus Christ the Son of God command it? It is inexpressibly important to know why you believe what you believe, because, I'll give you a heads up, the devil will send people to try to snatch those beliefs and morals from you, and you have to be ready to defend your faith from vicious wolves disguised as harmless sheep (Matthew 7:15).

Ask a godly, Christian adult—maybe even an elderly person— to share a time with you where they put their trust in the Lord (or, when they wish they would have put their trust in the Lord). Sometimes it's hard to let go of our grip on life, because we have the misconception that our world will come crashing down after we let go of the handle. But, you know something? God grabs that handle right from us, and our world does come crashing down—because it's not our world anymore. It's God's.

FOOD FOR THOUGHT...

1. What do you think the problem is with believing that God used evolution instead of Creation?

   Evolution says there is no God: If there is no God, then where do we go when we die? There is no hope if there is no God.
   —JASON, AGE 13

2. What do you think God thinks when others change up His Word?

   I think He's disappointed because He made us and gave us the Bible for a reason, and it really shouldn't be changed.
   —NAOMI, AGE 11

3. What makes it hard for you to surrender everything to God?

   Our pride is what makes it hard to surrender everything to God.
   —CASSIE, AGE 12

4. What are some of the fears that hinder people from placing their lives in God's hands?

   The fear of what others will think of them. —JOE, AGE 17

5. What makes God so trustworthy?

   He will protect you. —ESME, AGE 9

CHAPTER 7
Prophecy

BIRTH OF THE KING

ISAIAH 9:1-7, MATTHEW 1:18-25

The prophet Isaiah wrote out the Lord's new message to the people of Judah. He scratched his head in confusion over what it meant:

> *"The people who walk in darkness will see a great light. For those who live in a land of deep darkness, a light will shine. You will enlarge the nation of Israel, and its people will rejoice. They will rejoice before you as people rejoice at the harvest and like warriors dividing the plunder."* (Isaiah 9:2-3)

Something magnificent was going to happen—something so wonderful that it would call for celebration! Isaiah continued writing the words that the Lord spoke to him. Again and again, each new phrase gave some sign of hope and improvement to the crumbling kingdom of Judah. The prophet wondered what on earth could be so amazing that it could change the desolate state of life that the Judeans had been enduring due to their sins. Even on sunny days, the clouds seemed to droop in a gloomy, gray manner. The chosen people had sinned against God and His laws, and now they were facing the punishment. Each day, the Jews lived in sheer horror with the fear that, perhaps, their hometown would be plundered again—and they would be the ones having to go into exile this time.

"For unto us a child is born, unto us a son is given: and the government shall be upon his shoulder: and his name shall be called Wonderful, Counsellor, The mighty God, The everlasting Father, The Prince of Peace." (Isaiah 9:6 KJV)

A child! That caught Isaiah by surprise. A child was going to fix the downfallen kingdom of Judah? A child was going to make life better? The government will be on a child's shoulders? He could hardly believe his own writing.

"His government and its peace will never end. He will rule with fairness and justice from the throne of his ancestor David for all eternity. The passionate commitment of the Lord of Heaven's Armies will make this happen!" (Isaiah 9:7)

The child was going to be a king! He would bring peace to Judah and sit on King David's throne as the ruler. He would uphold justice and righteousness—Judah's enemies were finally going to get what they deserved: punishment. Or, did it? Isaiah had been a prophet long enough to know that, sometimes, the prophecies that God would reveal could possibly mean something other than what they sound like. *But it all sounds so good!* thought Isaiah.

God had called the child *Wonderful, Counsellor, The mighty God, The everlasting Father,* and *The Prince of Peace.* Such names for such a miracle from God! Such names for the redeemer of the Judeans! Could this king have anything to do with the child who the Lord had told Isaiah about before?

"...the Lord himself will give you the sign. Look! The virgin will conceive a child! She will give birth to a son and will call him Immanuel (which means 'God is with us')..." (Isaiah 7:14)

Knowing God, Isaiah wondered if there might be some connection between the messages. But what did all this mean?

About seven hundred years later...

Jesus was born to young Mary and her husband, Joseph. An angel came to Joseph and said, *"And she* [Mary] *will have a son, and you are to name him Jesus, for he will save his people from their sins."* (Matthew 1:21; brackets mine). The Word says that, *"All of this occurred to fulfill the Lord's message through his prophet: "Look! The virgin will conceive a child! She will give birth to a son, and they will call him Immanuel, which means 'God is with us.'"* (Matthew 1:22-23). Sound familiar? Had Isaiah still been alive, he sure would have thought so!

When Jesus grew up into a man, he did not sit on a throne as a king of Judah, yet he was the King. He did not destroy Judah's enemies, rather he paved the way for sinners and Gentiles (people who aren't Jews) to be saved from eternal life in hell. That's true justice. Everyone has a chance. He died and came back to life so that all, both Jews and the Gentiles alike, could have a chance to accept Him as the King of their life, so that they could have eternal life in heaven with the Lord. No, He did not make the glamorous entrance to the world that people thought He would. And no, He didn't look like royalty or like a king. Yet, Jesus fulfilled the prophecies. God's ways are higher than man's. Jesus came into the world as a little baby boy sleeping in a feeding box, died for the sins of all, and left—leaving all with the hopeful assurance that He will return someday—this time, like a King.

Wait Up!

Seven hundred years! I don't know if I could have waited that long. Actually, I know I couldn't have waited that long! The people of Isaiah's time were long dead when his prophecies about Jesus got fulfilled. Why? Why is God's timeline so different than ours? If I had been Isaiah receiving such an amazing, mysterious prophecy about a child who would become king and save Judah from the scary, horrible times that they were facing, I would have hoped to be alive around the time that it came to pass! Why don't we always get what we want *when* we want it? Why doesn't God always fulfill His words immediately? Why do we have to wait?

You and I both know waiting first-hand. We wait everyday! We wait for class to be over, we wait for the waiter to bring out our food, we wait for summer vacation. When we call someone on the phone, we wait for the person on the other line to pick up. When we're in a car, the driver has to wait at the red light until it turns green. As my three-year-old sister would say, "Waiting is *haaaaaard*." So why does God make us wait?

By now, you hopefully have realized how in-control God really is. He is in charge of everything that happens in the whole universe! Waiting is a part of the process that God uses in order to accomplish His plans. He knows past, present, and future, and, well, we don't. We may know bits and pieces of past, present, and possibilities of what might happen in the future (for example, my birthday was last month, today is a school day, and Easter is in a few weeks). But, ultimately, God knows everything that's ever gone on at any time. We already know that trusting God is a huge deal—it is so important to transfer the authority over our lives from ourselves to God. And, we hopefully already realize that He is trustworthy. Do you think we can trust God to know the right timing on things? Absolutely. He's an expert on all things.

Sometimes, especially as young people looking forward to being older, we tend to want to rush our whole lives ahead. We think, *If only I were in middle school/high school/college! If only I were done with this. If only I didn't have to endure that! If only I didn't have to face such-and-such. If only so-and-so were still here! If only I were old enough to get my driver's license! If only I could vote! If only I were married! If only I had a job! If only I could* ___. Then, we think we'll be happier, or everything will be better.

Naturally, people want to experience the better and happier things in life, and just skip all the bad times and the waiting times. But, if humans were in charge of timing in life rather than God, things would be a mess. But you should know: you see bad timing every day. People don't time their driving correctly, and they hit someone, or run a red light. People thoughtlessly make an unnecessary comment or crack a joke at a bad time. People ride roller coasters after lunch (that one is self-explanatory). People forget the time—and they leave box pizzas in the oven too long. They forget to feed the dogs. They forget their dentist's appointment. You get the idea. We think we know what's best for us when we actually don't. But God really does know what is best for us.

You've probably heard the popular phrase, "Patience is a virtue." Patience is not about how *easy* the waiting is, but about what our response is to the waiting process. We have the choice to be angry at God for making us wait and go through hard times, to fall away or lose hope when God makes us wait, and to ignore His commands and try another route. Yet, we also have the choice to trust God, even though we may not understand or see any good coming out of a waiting situation, and follow His commands and His lead. As Paul said, "I am torn between the two: I desire to depart and be with Christ, which is better by far..." (Philippians 1:23 NIV) Even the model Christian had to make this choice: to follow Christ.

Take Job, for example: God allowed Satan to inflict all kinds of hurt and sadness upon Job and to wreck the prosperous life he was living. All his animals, servants, and children died (not to mention, this all happened over the course of one short conversation). Painful boils covered Job's skin. Job's wife, undoubtedly affected by the tribulation, told him to "...Curse God and die" (Job 2:9 NIV). And to put the cherry on top of all of his troubles, Job's well-meaning friends, Eliphaz, Bildad, and Zophar, offered their unwelcome commentaries and advice on how his affliction came about because of his past sins—and they continued nearly the *whole time* that Job suffered.

That's what I call a hard waiting experience! And what was the point of God letting Him suffer and wait for the other end of the tunnel that whole time? A lot of times, when God makes us wait, it's because He has some lessons to teach us. Or sometimes, God wants His glory to shine through our situation. And, in some cases, like Job's, both! Job learned lessons about God's control over life, about God's powerfulness, about forgiveness, about standing up for the truth, and so much more. Job's response was a good one: In his words, "I will defend my integrity until I die" (Job 27:5). Job kept on living for God, and continued living as he did in Job 1:1: "He was blameless—a man of complete integrity. He feared God and stayed away from evil." In the end, God's glory shone when the Lord *doubled* Job's previous riches, gave him ten new children, and a long, full remainder of his life (he lived to a solid age over 140).

So, what do we do while we wait? Serve God. Serve others. Follow Job's example of fearing God, staying away from evil and walking blamelessly and uprightly. No, like pretty much every other worthwhile endeavor in life, doing this isn't easy. It is really actually quite hard. Being patient to see God's hand at work in your life is hard. Being patient to make it to the end of a tough time is hard. Being patient to grow up is hard. Being patient for the cookies to come out of the oven is hard! All waiting is hard; nevertheless, it is a blessing.

Wait, so after talking about how hard waiting is and how awful it can be, you're going to tell me that waiting time is a blessing?! Waiting time certainly can be a blessing! Remember, God is in control, and His plans are in our best interest. So, if He's got us waiting, then there must be something good in it for us.

God will sometimes use waiting as a means to keep us from harm. Maybe Karen is running thirty minutes late for a birthday party after waiting for her older brother to get ready to drive her there, but later she finds out that if they had left at the right time, they could have been in the middle of a huge car pile-up. Waiting can be a gift—a time of learning. Maybe Casey just moved to a new state, and he is having trouble making new friends. Maybe God wants to teach him in this waiting time to befriend his family first, before seeking outside buddies. Waiting can prepare us for what we're waiting for. Hopefully, you are getting the gist of the idea. No matter what waiting we may need to endure, or whatever measure of patience we may need to exercise, God is in control of life. We can trust that we're not waiting in vain.

Now, not all waiting is hard. Maybe you can hardly wait to go to college—yet, grade school and high school can be fun, memory-making, rewarding experiences. Maybe you think nothing could be more fun that arriving at the vacation destination you've been talking about for weeks—however, the car trip full of games, reading *The Greatest Book You've Never Read*, and seeing all sorts of different states does put up some pretty good competition against it. Maybe I am super excited about getting this book published, but I do enjoy the writing process. We'd better not miss the present because we're too busy looking at all the bad things about our situation or at all of the disadvantages. *But if only I had a car! Then I would be happy.* Maybe, but you'd have a lot more expenses than you do at the moment. There will always be pro's and con's in life, but we should ultimately strive to live by those last words in Nehemiah 8:10: "…Don't be dejected and sad, for the joy of the Lord is your strength!" Enjoy the wait. You may find that the "wait" you are in is really not much of a wait after all.

RETURN OF THE KING

BASED ON REVELATION 1:1-3,9; REVELATION 21-22

John, follower of Jesus, walked the sandy beaches of the island Patmos. Exile did leave plenty of time for such activities. As he walked along, deep in thought, an angel of the Lord appeared.

"John, servant of the Most High God," the angel said, "I have something to tell you. The time has come."

The angel then began to show things that John could have never believed, had he not witnessed it with his own eyes. Some things were wonderful and exciting, and some things were horrendous and terrifying. The angel of the Lord was showing John the fate of the world—the End Times.

John stood aghast as he saw the evil and wickedness to come. How could the people of the earth stray so far from righteousness and truth? Yes, there were tough, horrible times ahead. But, he began to see how everything fell into place. Many mysteries still remained about why, when, and how all this would take place. John also witnessed the incredible sights of the eternal future of the world *after* God destroyed the earth and the wickedness within it. That's where the good part began—and where this story begins.

"This is so...it's... it's so... so... amazing!" John stuttered in awe. Before his very eyes stood a display he would never, not in a million years, forget. The old earth, the sea, and the old heaven were gone—destroyed. But now, John beheld the new heaven and the new earth, as well as a New Jerusalem, or Holy City. The Holy City slowly lowered from above in the clouds, coming out of heaven from God, and John began to tremble.

"The new Jerusalem!" John cried. The ornate, lavish beauty of the town reminded him of a bride on her wedding day. Suddenly, the sound waves rippled with a resounding noise: the very voice of God.

Coming from the throne, the Lord said, "The place where I live I will now share with my people. I myself will live with you in this place. You will be My people, and I, your God. There will be no hurt, no sadness, no trouble, no pain, no death here in this new world. I got rid of the old system from the past earth—now, *I am making everything new* (Revelation 21:5)!" God smiled at John.

"Write down what I am saying, John. My words are true; they are trustworthy."

"It is finished! I am the Alpha and the Omega—the Beginning and the End. (Revelation 21:6) Whoever is thirsty, come to the fountain—you can have living water, free of charge. The people who are victorious in their life on the old earth will get all of this," He said, motioning to the new heaven, new earth, and the Holy City, "and they will be My children—My family! And I, the Lord, will be their God. But those wicked people of the old world have reached their final, eternal fate: the Lake of Fire. All of those who perverted the ways of God, who pursued evil, who loved the way of the world—burning sulfur is the only thing they will get."

A new angel showed up and asked John, "Would you like to see the Holy City?" He whisked his hand up towards the glorious sight. All John could do was nod his head to say, *"Of course I would! This is astounding!"* But he was so awestruck that he could hardly move. They went to the top of a towering mountain, where they could see the City with a perfect view.

"Wow! Look at the colors…I've never seen so many in one place! Colors I never knew existed! Oh, look how many gates there are! Look at this city!" John's eyes followed the long, walls, looking at every ornate contour in His Master's handiwork. "Look how tall and wide this City is!"

The angel whipped out a long, golden ruler. "To be exact, it is precisely…" He measured the length. "…12,000 stadia by 12,000 stadia, considering that it is square-shaped, and…." He measured the thickness of the wall. "The wall is 144 cubits thick. The foundations and walls are made of precious stones as you can see here," he pointed to the bright prisms of color which shone like auroras.

"Through the twelve pearl gates—which, by the way, are made of one single pearl each—you get a great view of the pure gold streets."

Peeking through the gates, John marveled at every sight. But he noticed that some certain things were missing. *Where is the temple?* he thought. But then, he quickly realized, *The Lord God is the temple of this new City!* The City did not have a sun or moon, because the Lord was the one who gave light to this place through His glory. The gates would always remain open, because there was no need to keep anyone out. *"Nothing evil will be allowed to enter, nor anyone who practices shameful idolatry and dishonesty— but only those whose names are written in the Lamb's Book of Life"* (Revelation 21:27).

A clear river, otherwise known as the water of life, raced through a garden, and, as the angel tour guide brought John to a tree, he said, "Here is the tree of life." Twelve different kinds of fruits hung from its branches. "The tree's leaves have medicinal value—they are for healing nations. God's throne will be in the city, and we, His servants, will serve Him. We will see His face! We will have His name on our foreheads. *And there will be no night there—no need for lamps or sun—for the Lord God will shine on them. And they will reign forever and ever* (Revelation 22:5)."

John listened intently as the angel went on to tell him, "All of these words that I have said to you are indeed truthful and trust-worthy. God, who was also the divine inspiration of the prophets, sent me to tell you these things, because they must happen soon."

The Lord then spoke, *"Look, I am coming soon* (Revelation 22:7)! Those who keep and believe the prophecies in this scroll are blessed!" Overwhelmed by the glory and splendor, John bowed down to worship the angel.

"*Stop!* What are you doing?" cried the angel. "Don't worship me! I'm just another servant of God, like you! Worship the Lord!" John got up on his feet. "Oh, and one more thing—don't seal this scroll up, because these End Times are coming soon. Very soon."

Still astounded, John finished up writing his Patmos vision. The last thing He had seen was Jesus, inviting those who are willing to live for Him to the Holy City. "*Look, I am coming soon, bringing my reward with me to repay all people according to their deeds. I am the Alpha and the Omega, the First and the Last, the Beginning and the End* (Revelation 22:12-13). Those who cleanse themselves from impurities and sinfulness are blessed, and they are the ones whom I will allow to enter the glorious Holy City! The wicked people who forsake God and His ways are the ones who will be outside, not permitted to enter. *I, Jesus, have sent my angel to give you this message for the churches. I am both the source of David and the heir to his throne. I am the bright morning star*" (Revelation 22:16).

John wrote, "Nobody should add or take away from these scrolls. Whoever does will be subject to severe punishment, including the removal of their share in the tree of life and Holy City. *He who is the faithful witness to all these things says, "Yes I am coming soon!"*

Amen! Come, Lord Jesus!

May the grace of the Lord Jesus be with God's holy people" (Revelation 22:20-21).

READY OR… NOT!

Did you hear that? He's coming soon. Very soon! Are you ready to stand before God? Are you ready to be admitted into the Holy City? The new heaven, the new earth, and the New Jerusalem sound like amazing places. But, as you can see, the admittance is conditional—not everybody gets in. Not everybody gets to enter. Not everybody will have an eternal life of happiness. The only alternative to this life of joy with the Lord is, well, "...the fiery lake of burning sulfur" (Revelation 21:8).

As believers and followers of Christ, we should look forward to His coming and getting to be with Him. However, especially for us young people, the thought of Jesus coming back so soon can sound a little less than thrilling. I know that I've thought, "Now hold on a second! I am excited to get to see Jesus and go to be with Him and all, but what about getting to experience the cool things about life on earth? Can't He maybe come a while *after* that?" Come on, you know that we've *all* thought that. What about graduating? Going to college? Becoming a certified neurosurgeon? Getting married? Having a family? A career? Becoming president? Climbing Mount Everest? What I'd never really thought of was that God "...knows the secrets of every heart," (Psalm 44:21), and He knows our thoughts and desires, even the ones we haven't told anybody about. So, don't you think we can trust Him to have thought this whole future heaven/earth/Holy City through? While we don't know every juicy little detail of the things God has in store for us, we know that it will be great! Besides, the same God who created the earth and the life in it that we may have trouble parting with—He's the same God who's creating this new place!

We know He's coming soon. How soon? Tomorrow soon? Next Friday soon? Next December soon? Next decade? 3013? Maybe... and, maybe not. Jesus tells us that nobody (including Himself) knows when He will be returning (Mark 13:32). Only the Father knows—which is why we have to be prepared. Right now is our chance to accept and live for Christ and store up for ourselves treasures in heaven. When He comes back, there will be no time to change or undo or redo or accept or believe. Everyone will believe and admit to the fact that Jesus is Lord once He comes back—but not everybody will enter into the Kingdom of heaven. There will, sadly enough, be people who will be thrown into their devastating destiny of the Lake of fire, and they will never get out. Once we stand before God on the "…judgment day…" (Matthew 12:36) we are past the "last chance." We will have to give a reason and explain ourselves for every single little "meaningless" thing we've ever said. What will you say?

When was the last time you asked yourself, "What does my spiritual person look like?" Maybe a little scrawny, starved, or sick? Or perhaps fit, active, and healthy? We need to make sure that we are not only eating our spiritual food daily, but that we are growing in our relationship with Christ and changing from our sinful habits and ways. That's what food does—help us grow and give us nutritional benefits. It is absolutely crucial to maintain our spiritual person. After all, what if Jesus came back now? Would He catch us at a bad time?

Seven Reasons We Are Hesitant to Evangelize

What are we going to do with this "waiting time" until Jesus's return? There is, of course, no time to waste. There are people out there who don't know the good news of Christ. There are people out there who haven't accepted Jesus. There are people who claim to have accepted Jesus, but they don't show it with their lifestyle. There are people like this everywhere—maybe in your very family. What are we waiting for? We've got work to do!

"...I have been given all authority in heaven and on earth. Therefore, go and make disciples of all the nations, baptizing them in the name of the Father and the Son and the Holy Spirit. Teach these new disciples to obey all the commands I have given you. And be sure of this: I am with you always, even to the end of the age." (Matthew 28:17-20). This famous command Jesus gave, known as the Great Commission, beckons us to go tell the world about Christ. A lot of us are hesitant to share the Gospel, maybe for one or more of the following possible reasons:

1. We think or assume that a certain person is already a Christian.
2. We think some one else has or will do it.
3. We don't want to get a reputation for being a goody goody, preachy converter.
4. We don't want to come off as "religious" or pushy.
5. We have problems going on in our own lives. Once we've conquered our struggles and problems, and we are spiritually "intact," *then* maybe we'll share.
6. We're not the social type.
7. We don't want to offend or "judge."

TIME IS TICKING

Suppose there was a time bomb in a building full of people, and you, being a member of the bomb squad, had the job of getting the people to evacuate the building. Inside the building, you walked up to a girl (pretend it was me) sitting on a comfy chair, sipping a delicious smoothie from Tropical Smoothie Café (now that is my idea of relaxation!).

You started out casually, "Hey, how's it going? Tropical Smoothie—yum. What kind is that? Oh, Peanut Butter Cup? Mmm." After an awkward pause, you continue, "So, um, no pressure or anything, but, like, uh, there's a bomb in here, so if you want to, or if you feel like it or something, I mean, you can leave the building. Totally your call, though," you told me. Then you leisurely strolled away. Wait, no, that's not what happened. Rewind.

Inside the building, you walked up to me, sitting on a comfy chair, sipping my smoothie.

"Quick, there's a bomb inside this building! You have to get out, before it blows!" Pretend I promptly pulled out a cockroach suit from my brief case (because, obviously, I always carry around a briefcase with a cockroach suit inside). As I put it on over my smoothie-stained clothes, you began to wonder what was going on there.

Going along with the analogy, I confidently explained to you, "This is my cockroach suit. I hear cockroaches survive the worst of bomb explosions, so I can keep sitting here sipping my smoothie in this cockroach suit. Not a hair on my head will get burnt!"

With a sigh, you said, "You know what? That's okay. This cockroach suit is your idea of "safe," and that's fine. My "safe" is outside the building, but I think both of us will be just fine. We'll just reach safety in different ways. Have a nice day." And with that, you walked away.

No, no, I don't think that was the right way, either. If there *was* a bomb inside of a building, you would run around, yelling for people to evacuate, not wanting to leave a person behind. You would go to all measures to make sure that, as the bomb squad member, you execute your job effectively and everyone is out of the building safe and sound (this being said, you would swiftly escort me, my cockroach suit, and my smoothie out of the building). Why aren't we scrambling around warning others of the bomb? Saving them through the good news of Jesus's love and salvation? There is only one way–one "safe"—and that is through the salvation of Jesus. Don't leave anyone behind—we have to tell the good news!

EVERY MAN FOR HIMSELF

Now...as not everyone will get to enter the marvelous Holy City, there is the other fate, found to be the destiny of many—the Lake of Fire, which is the devil's fate as well, according to Revelation 20:10. Who goes to the Lake of Fire? Revelation 21:8 tells us that the wicked go to this horrible place. Those who practice evil do not have admission into the new place where God will reign. There will, forever, be a chasm between them and God—one that will never, ever, in all of eternity, be closed. It is a sad, terrible thing—which is why we should not only warn others so that they don't have this dark destiny, but we should keep our hearts and lives in check and live every moment as if it were our last.

Most of us, if we knew we were living our last day, would want to leave a mark of love on the lives of those around us. We'd want to leave behind a good memory of ourselves. When you think about it, we really don't know when our last moment is, or when Jesus is coming back. Today, you could very well be living your last moments. The most important thing to remember is that we are humans with a sinful human nature and a wicked heart in a fallen, twisted world, and we can only be saved by the grace of God. Christ is the only way. No cockroach suits, no good works, no other religions will save us from destruction. Have you accepted Christ? (More on salvation in Chapter 12)

By looking at our hearts, minds, actions, and overall lives, can people tell that we're God's sons and daughters? Salvation and the Christian path of life is "every man (or woman) for himself (herself)." *But my mom is a Christian.* Sorry. That doesn't make you one. *But my dad is a really good guy.* That doesn't make you a really good guy, either. God wants you. He wants your life. He doesn't want your life via your reputation as the son or daughter of the Christian lady and that really good guy. The best way to give ourselves a check—an attitude check, action check, thought check, heart check, anything check—is by putting ourselves side-by-side to the ultimate standard: Jesus. Are we serving like Jesus did? Are we loving others like Jesus did? Are we talking to the Father, as Jesus did?

This way of life—living every moment in preparation for Jesus's return—is unpopular, even among some professing Christians. Be a trendsetter. Dare to be different. Stand out from the crowd. This isn't about being popular (or about using every cliché in the catch-phrase dictionary, for that matter): it's about reaching for the grand prize, which is so much more worth it that the little bit of praise we may get on earth for "popularity." As the apostle Paul said in 1 Corinthians 9:24 (NIV), "…Run in such a way as to get the prize."

So the prophecy in the Bible is really actually relevant to today, huh? Yes, and not only that, but, as stated before, everything in the Bible is there for a reason. Many prophecies lead to historical clarification, proof of legitimacy of the Bible, proof of the Bible's accuracy, proof of Jesus being the Son of God, proof of God's loving faithfulness to His people by following through with His words, and so much more. God's Word is alive! He has never forsaken us, nor will He ever. He didn't leave us with an outdated document. Even if someone stranded us on a desert island with a Bible, concordance, commentaries, studies, theological books, etc., and they left us there for fifty years, we could never, not in a million years, discover everything there is to know about God, the Bible, life, or the meaning of His Words. There is so much to learn in His Word, so let's seize the day and learn all we can!

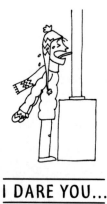

I DARE YOU...

Find a story about someone who had to wait on God's timing and benefited from the results. Maybe a missionary story, a family story, a friend's story, or even your own! Share how that story has impacted you with someone who needs to hear it.

If you have accepted Jesus into your heart as your Lord and Savior, evangelize! Tell others the good news of Christ. Want a conversation starter? Hand out tracts at events or recreational centers (information on tracts in the Resources section at the back of the book). One fun way to perk others' attention is to wear Christian t-shirts. Sharing the gospel isn't condemning people or saying, "You're going to hell!" and hoping that works. It's sharing about God's personal love for that individual and letting God work on that person's heart to make the decision to follow Christ. We can't convert people. God's the one who does the converting. See the recommendations at the back of the book for witnessing resources.

FOOD FOR THOUGHT...

1. When is it hardest for you to wait?

   When I am in line for a roller coaster ride. —RACHEL, AGE 10

2. Name a situation when you saw that God's timing was better than yours.

   I was debating on confronting one of my friends about a certain situation on how she had acted. I was asking the Lord if I should or if it was the right time... I would have liked to confront her right then but the Lord kept telling me no. So I gave Him the whole situation and asked that His timing would take place that He would make a way for me to talk to her about it. So I waited and confronted her later about it and I'm so glad that I waited because I found out some things had been going on and I just would have made it worse. I could've lost her as a friend and I would've lost an opportunity to share God's Word with her. —TAYLOR, AGE 16

3. Why should we, as believers, look forward to Christ's return?

The world will become perfect. There will be no sin, pain, or death. There will be no persecution and we will see how God conquers evil! We will get to see Jesus face to face, and praise Him forever! —HANNAH, AGE 15

4. What keeps you from (or makes you hesitant about) evangelizing to others?

The fear that people will look down on me as stupid and begin treating me like that. —AUSTIN, AGE 17

5. What are your personal duties to God as you wait for Christ to return?

Sharing the good news of Christ! —JAMES, AGE 11

CHAPTER 8
Interviews

{ THE HISTORY IN THE MAKING CHANNEL }
Gospel Hour with Mr. Host:
EXCLUSIVE INTERVIEW
~ WITH MATTHEW ~
ON THE SERMON ON THE MOUNT

BASED ON THE BOOK OF MATTHEW; MATTHEW 5, 6, 7

Behind-the-scenes interview of one of Jesus's twelve disciples like you've never seen before!

Keep your eyes open for Matthew's new book, released in one year: *Matthew*! Interview done by Mr. Host, courtesy of *History In the Making* channel. Thanks to all of those who made this interview possible.

Mr. Host: What is it like to be one of Jesus's twelve disciples?

MATTHEW: I never thought I, a former tax-collector, would be following God's own Son, the Messiah, around, witnessing the miracles he performs, understanding life in such a clear way, and getting such insight into God's character. I have to say, it humbles me.

Mr. Host: What do you think when people condemn Jesus for hanging out with people like you—the tax-collectors and sinners?

MATTHEW: They're right to call us sinners. What I've learned from Jesus is that we are all sinners, and we don't deserve to live, much less do we deserve a gracious God and His blessings. Jesus speaks of His Father in a way I had never known God before. He is kind, compassionate, and He wants to help us and save us. Jesus is the Son of God, and He is here to bring hope and love to the sinners. In the Messiah's own words, "Healthy people don't need a doctor—sick people do" (Matthew 9:12). If only those who condemned the Master knew that.

Mr. Host: What is the most breathtaking miracle you've witnessed so far?

MATTHEW: I don't know that I can call any one miracle more breathtaking than another! It is incredible to witness the authority that God gave His Son. Whenever He teaches, people swarm in to be healed and cleansed from various diseases and illnesses (Matthew 4:23). Whether it's leprosy, blindness, or any other kind of ailment, sometimes I'm left astounded at the faith of some of these people. But always, I'm left in awe of Jesus's mercifulness and willingness.

Mr. Host: Tell us a little about the Sermon on the Mount.

MATTHEW: A little?! We could talk about the Sermon on the Mount all day—no, all month! There's tons to cover!

Mr. Host: Okay, tell us a lot about the Sermon on the Mount. What are the "Beatitudes?"

MATTHEW: Jesus started out by telling the crowd about the rewards of possessing certain character traits and attitudes. The name gives the gist of the message: they are the "attitudes" you want to "be." The Master gave the Beatitudes to encourage His followers to continue their journey, because their eternal reward will be good. I learned that, even when people insult you, mock you, and persecute you, we should count ourselves blessed, because God will reward us well in heaven. The prophets of long ago, such as Isaiah and Jeremiah, had to endure such trials in their day and age.

Mr. Host: Jesus really ruffled some feathers when He began making changes on the Law of Moses. What do you think about that?

MATTHEW: Hang on, now—Jesus wasn't changing the Law or the Ten Commandments. He covered that in His message. He said, "Don't misunderstand why I have come. I did not come to abolish the law of Moses or the writings of the prophets. No, I came to accomplish their purpose. I tell you the truth, until heaven and earth disappear, not even the smallest detail of God's law will disappear until its purpose is achieved"

(Matthew 5:17-18). He even went on to speak of the consequences that follow the choice of setting the Law aside! Not only did Jesus come to fulfill the Law, but he brought new meaning to it. Take the example He gave on the law against murder, for instance. It still stands that you shall not murder anyone. Killing is still a sin. However, Jesus furthered the meaning. Now, if anyone is angry with his brother or sister for no reason, that is counted as murder. The Law of Moses stated that for every eye hurt, there was to be an eye in return. For every tooth, a tooth, and for every life, a life. However, Jesus told the people that now, we are not to "...resist an evil person..." (Matthew 5:39). Instead, we are to give that evil person the extra-mile treatment. An enemy Roman soldier asks you to walk a mile with him? Go ahead and walk two miles with him. He slaps you on one cheek? Turn your face to let him slap the other. He wants your shirt? Give him your cloak, as an extra.

Mr. Host: Last question. Tell us about the Lord's Prayer.

MATTHEW: Ah, yes, the Lord's Prayer. You see, many people, such as the Pharisees and Sadducees, like to ramble on and show off their so-called "holiness" or "spirituality" and excessive wordiness in their melodramatic prayer shows. They want people to see them and be impressed by them. God doesn't like that. It's what the pagans do—they think that if they are wordy enough, maybe their god (or gods) will listen to them. With the One True God, however, things are different. He wants you to really *talk* to Him—not show-off for people by pretending to talk to Him. In fact, Jesus told the people to go into a quiet place—like their rooms—shut the door, and pray. God sees what happens in secret. God knows your needs before you even tell Him. Jesus gave the people a sample prayer so they could know what true prayer looks like. Looking at the time here, I can see that this show's almost up, but I'll leave you the reference to the prayer: Matthew 6:9-15. You can find it in my soon-to-be-released book, *Matthew*, as well. I encourage everyone to read the Lord's Prayer.

Mr. Host: Thanks, Matt. It's been great talking with you. Come back again soon.

MATTHEW: I will. Thanks, guys!

You heard it here on this special episode of the *Gospel Hour* first, folks: the exclusive interview with Matthew on the Sermon on the Mount! Come back next week for the final episode of the epic reality TV show of two castaway teams faced with natural disasters at their most disastrous: *Joel: Locust Survival*. Who will get sent home this week? Next up, *Gospel Hour*'s exclusive, on-camera interview with Jesus's disciple. John, like never seen before! You're watching the *History In the Making* channel.

The Best Sermon Ever Given on a Mountain

It's incredible how a message given so long ago could be so relevant today. The topics that Jesus covers in the Sermon on the Mount are real life subjects and troubles that come up in everyday life! Those standards He set for us aren't dated. In fact, just read Matthew 5-7, and you may find that Jesus answers the questions you have right now! Full of encouragement, clarification, tips, and standards, there's no way I could fit a whole sermon on the Sermon on the Mount in a couple pages! I encourage you to venture into deep waters of the ocean of words we call the Bible, and read the Sermon for yourself. There are many good lessons we can learn. So, pause, take a break, and read the passage.

Wait, wait, wait—don't start reading yet! Before we read the Word of God or listen to a message from the Bible, we need to check our hearts and make sure they are teachable. Throughout the book of Proverbs, there are many verses saying that those who take correction and listen to counsel are blessed (not to mention, wise). Is your heart willing to accept correction right now, even if the Lord convicts you of something bad or even *embarrassingly* bad that you need to change in your life? Are you willing to take Jesus's counsel and practice what you've learned, even if it means taking an unpopular route and standing out from the crowd?

A heart than shuns correction or teaching is a symptom of the chronic disease called pride. God corrects us because He loves us. He doesn't want us to have to make the same mistake twice. He wants to give us counsel that will prevent "sickness." It's like He's giving us our spiritual vitamins—and boy, what an honor that is (Job 5:17)! Read Proverbs 16:20, 29:14, and 29:18. Proverbs 28:14 (NIV) states: "…whoever hardens their heart falls into trouble." Ooo, let's not. Jesus's teaching sounds way better.

Be the Saltiest Light You Can Be
MATTHEW 5:13-16

After the Beatitudes (which talks about all of the attitudes we should "be"), Jesus tells the people in Matthew 5:13-14 that "You are the salt of the earth… You are the light of the world." He spoke in parables (or stories) and analogies. In other words, He wasn't telling the crowd that they were, literally, the mineral salt.

Now, chances are, you probably know a few people that claim to be Christians, yet they act like everybody else. Christ just isn't very evident in their lives, actions, or conversations. It's disappointing to see that people, possibly even our own friends or family, are falsely advertising what Christianity is like. It's sending a message that causes a problem. The problem is that being a true Christian is not as easy as saying, "Yeah, I'm a Christian," or "Go Jesus! Whoo!" Salvation is definitely a free gift from God (Ephesians 2:8-9), and Jesus is definitely our free ticket to heaven, but Christianity is definitely not at all like booking a hotel room and then going on with life, forgetting all about it until the time comes for the trip.

As true, full-hearted followers of Jesus Christ, we shouldn't settle for a lifestyle of wishy-washy Christianity. We should be the salt and the light of the world—in other words, the most flavorful and brightest in the world. Christ's love and joy should be so obvious in our lives, actions, and words that people watch us and say, "What is it about Tyler? There's something different about him," and "There's just something about Anna. It's like the room lights up when she walks through the door!" When people meet someone so salty and bright, they're often drawn to them, because the presence of Jesus draws others.

Don't be deceived—true Christianity is not necessarily going to make you happy all the time or make you popular; in fact, many times Christians have had to endure deep pains, hurts, and rejection for the sake of Christ. Think of famous Christians like the ten Boom family, George Müller, and John Bunyan. They didn't have a massive group of buddies gathered around them, gushing over their Christian values and virtues, nor did they have lives that would be considered easy, fun, or happy. Yet, there was something different about them—something that made them stand out, and their stories continue to inspire people today. Consider, for instance, the ten Booms—after hiding Jews during World War II, they were sent to concentration camps, one of which they had to sleep in a flea-infested barrack. Yet, they continued to show love, thankfulness, joy, and share about Jesus with those around them. Talk about living boldly for Christ! The nutshell version of Jesus's analogy with salt and light would probably say, "Don't hide that you're my followers! Make it obvious!"

CONVICTED OF ANGER
MATTHEW 5:21-26

I don't know about you, but I find Jesus's talk on meaningless anger being the equivalent of murder a little... tough to swallow. I mean, come on, if I'm mad at my sister just because, that is not so bad, right? Right? Well, Jesus tells otherwise. He says that if you are "... angry with [your] brother without a cause [you] shall be in danger of the judgment..." (Matthew 5:22 NKJV; brackets mine). Okay, so it is a little bad. Okay, a lot bad. But there's more.

Jesus said that anyone who calls his brother (or sister) a fool "... shall be in danger of hell fire" (Matthew 5:22 NKJV). Name calling may have never seemed like such a big deal until now. So then, the Lord tells us that we should ask for forgiveness for offenses our brother (or sister) may have against us—before we talk to God. If we don't repent, we shouldn't be surprised to find a brick wall in our communication with the Lord. First, make things right—that means tossing pride in the trashcan and pulling out one of our greatest weapons: humility. Then, we can go talk to God and—hey, that brick wall's been knocked down. Well, how about that.

Jesus tells us that things get bad when we don't make up with our brothers and sisters quickly. After all, why should we wait a long time to apologize and let hard feelings settle in? Pride is usually the source of delayed apologies or forgiveness. In all love, we need to be the bigger person, as they say, in the situation. Walk in the mature, loving way that Jesus commands us to. He really does consider getting along with others to be a big deal. This applies to our brothers and sisters in Christ as well (otherwise known as the fellow believers around us—we Christians are all apart of God's family), so you're not off the hook if you're an only child! But let's not stop here—we have even more back up for Matthew 5:21-26.

1 John 2:11 says that "...anyone who hates another brother or sister is still living and walking in darkness. Such a person does not know the way to go, having been blinded by the darkness." Then, we read in 1 John 3:10 (NIV), "This is how we know who the children of God are and who the children of the devil are: Anyone who does not do what is right is not God's child, nor is anyone who does not love their brother and sister." You may be shocked to find the apostle Paul calling those who "do not love their brother and sister" the "children of the devil!" He didn't even say "those who hate their brother and sister"... he said those who "do not *love!*" Read 1 John 3:11-18 for expansion on the topic. The Bible certainly communicates loudly and clearly that we must love. We absolutely must. We'd better not let anger get the best of us. We'd better not hate our neighbor. We'd better steer clear of "not loving" our brothers and sisters. It's as bad as murder.

Don't Be In a Hurry to Worry
MATTHEW 6:25-34

It is true that worrying never helped anybody—a practical life truth taught by Jesus in none other than (you guessed it) the Sermon on the Mount. As we can see, the Bible definitely covers modern-day issues—yes, people back in Jesus's day worried, too! "Can all your worries add a single moment to your life?" (Matthew 6:27). Well, when you put it that way...

Why do we worry about things when God is in control? He's the one that provides for us. He's the one that takes care of us. As Jesus put it, "Look at the birds. They don't plant or harvest or store food in barns, for your heavenly Father feeds them. And aren't you far more valuable to him than they are?" (Matthew 6:26). God takes care of the birds—those with less value than us—but we don't trust Him to take care of us, His children? The ones He sent His Son to die for? I'm starting to think worry may be a lack of trust. If we trusted God so much, we wouldn't have anything to worry about.

The birds, the flowers, and the people of this earth all have the same Maker and the same Caretaker. If God is taking care of the least important members of this planet with such precise care, just imagine the measures He takes to care for you and me! "These things dominate the thoughts of unbelievers, but your heavenly Father already knows all your needs" (Matthew 6:32). He knows what we need! Don't you feel blessed to have woken up this morning? To be living another day? We owe all the thanks to God for providing and caring for us throughout our lives, even if others did not.

Besides the fact that distrust is unhealthy, worrying has physically unhealthy side effects. It's just not good for us! Worrying also sticks to one's reputation—nobody enjoys hanging out with a person who is constantly neck-deep in worry. And, worry is distracting. It takes our mind off of enjoying the day, focusing on the Lord, or concentrating on our tasks. Jesus tells us, "So don't worry about tomorrow, for tomorrow will bring its own worries. Today's trouble is enough for today" (Matthew 6:34). Besides, worrying never did help anyone.

HYPOCRITES ANONYMOUS
MATTHEW 7:1-5

Nobody likes being criticized or judged. Yet, as much as we dislike being the victim of judgment, we are highly guilty of the sin ourselves. You know who you are, and you probably know who you've judged. We've all done it, y'all! Let's not disown the fact that we judged Mrs. Smith's parenting skills just yesterday, or that we thought that the new kid at youth group was stuck up because he didn't talk to anybody. Not to mention, we didn't think Oscar was a Christian because we heard from Corbin who heard from Natasha who heard from Simon who heard from Shaylee that he got kicked out of his old school back in second grade. Wait, hang on—Shaylee actually heard that from Sophie's older brother, Wayne. At least, we think that's what we heard...

Not to say that there aren't things that should change in the lives of those around us, but we have plenty of our own problems to deal with first. Jesus makes a very clear analogy in his sermon: "And why worry about a speck in your friend's eye when you have a log in your own? How can you think of saying to your friend, 'Let me help you get rid of that speck in your eye,' when you can't see past the log in your own eye? Hypocrite! First get rid of the log in your own eye; then you will see well enough to deal with the speck in your friend's eye" (Matthew 7:3-5).

The friend with the plank in his eye was trying to remove the other friend's speck. He didn't care to remove the entire log out of his own eye before removing the little splinter in the other's eye. He couldn't see what he was doing because of the huge piece of wood barricading his view. Jesus used such an outlandish, out-of-proportionally exaggerated example of the plank in the friend's eye to illustrate a profound point: the problems in his life were bigger than the problems he was noticing in his brother's life. That's called being a hypocrite—doing the exact thing that we preach against.

In other words, Amy shouldn't keep nagging her brother to do his homework if she hasn't done hers. Will shouldn't judge his schoolmates as "less Christian" than he is because they talk bad about Zach when all he ever does with his church friends is talk bad about Luis (not to mention, "less Christian" is a made-up term, because Christianity is not a gradient scale). Maggie needs to consider the pride in her own life before telling Josh that his behavior is prideful. Hypocrisy is just not fair. Jesus was stating a common sense principle—one which should be a universal truth.

Another reason not to judge is because it's like a boomerang—it comes right back at you. Jesus said, "Do not judge others, and you will not be judged. For you will be treated as you treat others. The standard you use in judging is the standard by which you will be judged" (Matthew 7:1-2). Wow—that gets complicated! So, if Lauren judges her cousin Morgan as a judgmental proud person, perhaps others will start feeling the same way about Lauren. The moral of the story: please—don't judge. It isn't our place. Let God do the judging (Romans 14:4,10).

{ THE HISTORY IN THE MAKING CHANNEL }
Gospel Hour with Mr. Host:
EXCLUSIVE INTERVIEW
~ WITH JOHN ~
ON BEING A SERVANT

THE BOOK OF JOHN

Behind-the-scenes interview of one of Jesus's twelve disciples like you've never seen before!

Keep your eyes open for John's epic trilogy, released this Spring: *The John Series* (made up of 1, 2, 3 John) (includes John's latest letter, *3 John*). Interview done by Mr. Host, courtesy of the *History In the Making* channel. Thanks to all of those who made this interview possible.

Mr. Host: Hi John! Good to have you in the studio with us. Things been good for you lately?

JOHN: Incredible! You wouldn't believe the miracles I've witnessed lately if I told you. God has been doing a powerful work in the fellowship of believers! But, that's not what we're here to talk about today, is it?

Mr. Host: Sadly, no. But, we would like an exclusive interview on that after your trilogy is released! I understand that it's been a couple years since Jesus ascended into heaven, leaving all with the hopeful promise of His return. Nevertheless, in order to kick off season 4 of The Gospels, *we'd like to hear about your ministry along with Jesus.*

JOHN: Well, that is a pretty long question to answer. As I wrote in my first book, *John,* "Jesus also did many other things. If they were all written down, I suppose the whole world could not contain the books that would be written" (John 21:25). But, in a nutshell, Jesus's ministry was serving.

Mr. Host: I understand that the idea of being a servant to others, including enemies, is not a popular idea. Could you give some examples of how Jesus demonstrated this idea of selfless serving to His disciples?

JOHN: Jesus was always serving. From the first day of his public ministry, when he turned water into wine at the wedding in Cana (John 2:1-11), to assisting some of the disciples with their fishing (John 21:1-14), there are hundreds of examples I could give. Yet, I think one of the most memorable acts of service that Jesus made was done serving us, His disciples.

We were having dinner with Jesus, when suddenly, He got up, filled a bowl with water, and began washing one of the disciples' feet! After one, He did another. And another. Eventually, He got to Simon Peter, who was reluctant. He asked Jesus if He was really going to wash his feet. Jesus told him that he would understand later. I clearly remember the bewildered look on Peter's face as he hurriedly jumped back and said, "No...you will never ever wash my feet!" (John 13:8). Jesus then explained to him that without being washed, he could not belong to Him. Upon hearing this, Peter scurried to a chair and pleaded that the Lord wash his hands and head while He was at it. Jesus then explained to Peter how he was already clean, but his feet got dirty as he walked, so he needed to be washed.

Jesus was setting a great example for us to follow. He was our Master, yet He made Himself as lowly as a servant for our sake. He humbly knelt down to wash the feet of those who were less than Him, considering our needs over His. He beckoned us to do the same to others, for we will be blessed if we do. He reminded us that no one is greater than God, so if God in the flesh can serve and love, then we certainly aren't too good or lofty to follow His example.

Not only that, but Jesus was making a huge statement on forgiveness when He washed our feet. You see, without His forgiveness—His cleansing us—we can have no part in the Lord. We need to accept His forgiveness and allow Him to wash us, because in our walk of life, our feet get dirty. When he told us to follow His example, He was also telling us to forgive others as He had forgiven us.

Mr. Host: Many times, with any publicity, there comes attention and glory. Not many people handle the limelight very well. How did Jesus handle all the fame?

JOHN: I recall Jesus Himself telling us, "If I were to testify on my own behalf, my testimony would not be valid. But someone else is also testifying about me, and I assure you that everything he says about me is true" (John 5:31-32). Jesus never puffed Himself up or became proud. He was clearly on earth for the sole purpose of doing the Lord's business. He also said, "Your approval means nothing to me... No wonder you can't believe! For you gladly honor each other, but you don't care about the honor that comes from the one who alone is God" (John 5:41,44). Jesus's ultimate glory came from His Father, God. That is all that mattered to Him, and it is all that should matter to us. What I learned in this message is that humans aren't good at giving glory. People are weak glory-givers. God, however, lavishes us with glory indescribable. Why, then, do we seek the glory of the people around us rather than God's? Jesus really brought that into light for me.

Mr. Host: I think we've got time for one more. Why should others want to serve?

JOHN: As followers of Jesus, we should strive to follow His example. Jesus told us, "There is no greater love than to lay down one's life for one's friends" (John 15:13). In order to show the ultimate climax of love, we must lay down our lives for others. To some, this may mean dying for others. Jesus understood that. But ultimately, we are called to lay down our lives for others by giving up our desires and letting go of our pride and, in some cases, dignity. We are then to serve them as if they and their needs and wants are greater than ours.

We are called to a difficult and unpopular narrow road. But, as my friend Luke put Jesus's words in his new book, *Luke*, "Love your enemies! Do good to them. Lend to them without expecting to be repaid. Then your reward from heaven will be very great, and you will truly be acting as children of the Most High, for he is kind to those who are unthankful and wicked" (Luke 6:35). This applies to everyone, not just our enemies. As followers of Christ, we are called to be servants!

Mr. Host: Great! We're all so inspired by your testimonies, and I'm sure our viewers are, as well. Thanks for coming in today, John! We'll contact you soon about an interview on the trilogy. We'll see you soon!

JOHN: It was a pleasure! I'll be expecting to hear from you. Thanks for having me!

You heard it here on this special episode of the *Gospel Hour* first, folks: the exclusive interview with John on being a servant. Come back this Sunday for a season premiere of the brand new miniseries, *Acts*, followed by an exclusive, on-camera interview with the apostle Paul, like never seen before! Next up, the *Simon Peter Says* game show! Who will win the Million Denarius Jackpot today? You're watching the *History In the Making* channel.

Someone Old, Someone New

Jesus, the King of kings and Lord of lords, washed His disciples' feet?! He brought Himself so low for the sake of a bunch of fallen, imperfect sinners. Jesus—the King of kings and Lord of lords—died for a bunch of people far below His rank who rejected Him. And we, humans with a sinful nature, have trouble patiently proving a listening ear to a stuttering toddler telling us about his favorite insect, willingly picking up the dirty laundry our siblings left on the floor, or even joyfully giving our time to someone else who wants to hang out with us when we could be doing other, more "important" things.

We shouldn't deny it. We consider ourselves to be the most important, a concept that happens to be the complete opposite of Philippians 2:3: "Don't be selfish; don't try to impress others. Be humble, thinking of others as better than yourselves." Selfish is what Jesus was not. He was *selfless*. He served. Why don't we have the servant's heart that He had? Is it possible to have such a ministry of service as Jesus had?

The answer is yes. In Matthew 19:26, Jesus says, "...with God everything is possible." Is it possible to have such a ministry of service as Jesus had by taking an easy way? The answer is no. Serving others—enemies and family members included—requires a lot of dying to self. As Galatians 2:20 says, "My old self has been crucified with Christ. It is no longer I who live, but Christ lives in me…" In order to serve with a pure heart, we need to nail all of our desires and pleasures to the cross with Jesus. We need to get rid of "the old man (or woman)" (who we were before we came to know Jesus), and put on "the new man (or woman)."

What did the "old man" want? He wanted to be lazy. He wanted to lounge around and be served. He wanted everything to be brought to him on his agenda. And, when his parents forced him to help out and serve, he sulked and half-heartedly worked, getting impatient at the slightest inconvenience. How do we overcome him? Inviting Jesus into your heart is a decision—and it's a great one to make. But then we must change our lives to fit with the commitment we made to follow Jesus. There is no way out of work—in fact, this is just the beginning of all the work required for serving!

PRIDE OVERRIDE

Surrendering our pride is one of the most crucial steps in becoming a servant. A servant?! No, that never was a very glamorous job. Yet, if our sinless, perfect, holy Savior could bring Himself down to the lowly position of "servant," then that is a perfect fit for us as His followers. When we surrender our pride, we forcefully stop thinking of ourselves as too good for a job…because we aren't. We need to start "…thinking of others as better than [ourselves]" (Philippians 2:3; brackets mine). That—I think—is where it gets a little painful.

My human nature tells me that I need to be looking out for number one and considering her to be the best. And, what about those people who really do consider themselves better than me? I'm supposed to let them be "right?" I'm not supposed to fight them?! This is where we put dying to self into practice. We may feel defeated inside—extremely annoyed, itching for justice, and maybe even angry. As Paul states in Philippians 1:21 (NIV), "For to me, to live is Christ and to die is gain." The NLT Bible gives us an interesting angle of this verse: "For to me, living means living for Christ, and dying is even better." Paul understood that the Christian walk involves living and dying—but, whichever he is doing, he considers an honor for Christ's sake. If you're having trouble getting into the swing of serving others joyfully… it may be time to die a little.

Put Me to Work

Servants are at the disposal of those around them of higher rank. Thank of the people around you in your life. Some of those probably include family, friends, schoolmates, church members, and teachers. Good—we know who our target audience is. Jesus had people, such as the leper, come up to Him and say, "…Lord… if you are willing…" (Matthew 8:2). And, of course, He always was willing to help them, as we should be. The clean jobs, the dirty jobs, the fun jobs, the boring jobs—we will do it all with a smile on our face, with a joyfully attitude, and with a humble approach. After all, we are representing Jesus. We never know when someone is observing us, wondering, "What makes that person, a Christian, so different from others? What do they have that I need?"

Wait, wait... did you say "fun jobs" somewhere in there? Serving can be... fun? Well, of course it can be fun! It isn't always fun, but it certainly can be! As my grandpa would tell my mom when she was a little girl, we should find something we enjoy in everything we do. Maybe Jackson dislikes building the fence outside, but he does look forward to painting it. Hailey doesn't prefer sweeping the floor, but she does sort of like to see how big she can make the pile of dust. Grayson doesn't like mowing the lawn, but he does like to see if he can beat his previous time. Find little things, in everything you do, that you enjoy. Find ways to serve others that you enjoy. Not to say that you won't have to serve in a way that you don't enjoy sometimes, but it is always nice to enjoy your work.

Serving others doesn't necessarily mean doing their chores (although that is an effective way to help); it simply means helping out where help is needed or wanted—even if it requires sacrifice on our part. Your aunt needs you to hold the baby for a while—just as you were about to go outside? Your mom wants help fixing sandwiches for dinner—even though you were doing your homework? You promised to help Nick study for the big test—that is, before McKenzie invited you to go bowling. But it's okay. As servants, we serve to the best of our ability—with a smile.

Smile

Obviously, it's hardest to smile when we're not enjoying ourselves. While there are plenty of fun ways to serve, sometimes—okay, a lot of times, serving can be boring and tiring. The Bible shows us that joyfulness is not just a resulting emotion that happens when we are having a good time—it's a choice. *I could be upset at having to do extra work for people who might not even pay me back—or, I could be joyfully doing my work with a smile because I know that I am pleasing the Lord.* Besides, as the apostle Peter puts it, "…If anyone serves, they should do so with the strength God provides, so that in all things God may be praised through Jesus Christ" (1 Peter 4:11 NIV).

Old Testament prophet Habakkuk chose wisely when he said, "…yet I *will* rejoice in the Lord! I *will* be joyful in the God of my salvation!" (Habakkuk 3:18; italics mine). What a decision to make! As believers, this is nothing we can't do. As the Word says in Nehemiah 8:10, "Don't be dejected and sad, for the joy of the Lord is your strength!" When we serve someone with real joy and a real smile on our face, we send a message to that person that says, "You are important (to me). You are worth the effort. I'm happy to do it." It also sends a message that we are happy to be Christ's followers doing His work.

Love will ultimately spring up out of our love for Christ and His commands. We want others to know and feel the love that God has for them, and we live that by serving them. Also, we never know who may be watching us, trying to decide whether or not they want to become one of Christ's followers, as well. As we serve, we should keep our audience in mind. While we should serve even when no one's watching and without expecting anything in return, let's face it: there are people watching and we do get something in return.

The people watching should see the love and joy of Christ radiating out of our every word, action, look, and smile. Someone may be watching, thinking, *Hmm, so this is what Christians are like, huh? Well, I want what Jenna has. She's just so pleasant to be around.* Then, others, possibly someone younger than you, might watch you and think, *Wow! Cody is so cool. He's just so nice. I want to be like that!*

And now, the moment we've all been waiting for: the unveiling of the prize. "…Those who are the greatest among you should take the lowest rank, and the leader should be like a servant" (Luke 22:26). Gather around, greatests and leaders! The prize, granted by Jesus Himself, is to, "…Come, you who are blessed by my Father, inherit the Kingdom prepared for you from the creation of the world" (Matthew 25:34). Why? What did we do to deserve that? According to the Lord, "…I was hungry, and you fed me. I was thirsty, and you gave me a drink. I was a stranger, and you invited me into your home. I was naked, and you gave me clothing. I was sick, and you cared for me. I was in prison, and you visited me" (Matthew 25:35-36).

Um… we did? Your response might like the response of the righteous, "No offense, Lord, but when exactly did we do any of these things for you?" Jesus gives the answer, "…I tell you the truth, when you did it to one of the least of these my brothers and sisters, you were doing it to me!" (Matthew 25:40). You mean, we *served?* Wow! What a reward! We were only trying to help little Jonah get better grades in Science class, but we ended up serving Jesus as well! We were only trying to shovel Mr. Bryant's snow covered driveway, but we actually served Jesus in the process! The road may be rough, but the destination we'll reach will be worth it!

Most people would agree that live TV and interviews are best and most interesting when they're not staged—when you're watching an actual story or occurrence. Most people would also agree that a great story is even better when it's a true story. The Bible, containing stories spanning over four thousand years in history, is completely true—no staging or fiction involved. You may have learned a virtuous lesson from a children's fable from a storybook when you were younger. The fictional stories of the runaway gingerbread boy and the boy who cried "Wolf!" seemed pretty relevant and "deep" back then. Now, as many of us young people start thinking about and entering teen and adulthood, we have another Book we can turn to for relevant, timeless lessons to teach us, inform us, correct us, convict us, and encourage us. The best part is, while we may outgrow Mother Goose, we'll never outgrow the Bible.

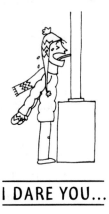

I DARE YOU...

Read Matthew 5-7 (also known as the Sermon on the Mount). Time to put your Bible reading/processing/analyzing skills to the test. Then, go find other verses in the Bible that back up what Jesus is saying. I'd recommend using a Bible website like www.biblegateway.com for searching. For you over-achievers, do a little Bible journaling on each "section" in the sermon. You'll learn a whole lot.

Pick a serving target for a set amount of time—like a week, two weeks, or (for those of you daring enough) a month. Don't tell them that they're your project—just do it. Serve them with everything you've got. Help them out. Practice the skills you learn from God's Word. You may be surprised that you benefit equally (or more than) the one served, because—here's a well-kept secret—serving can bring in loads of joy!

FOOD FOR THOUGHT...

1. What are some ways that you can show that you are a follower of Jesus?

*The truth is that there should not be a single area of our lives that doesn't loudly proclaim that we are a follower of Jesus. It should be evident in our every action and response. Jesus clearly said, "Follow Me, and I will make you become fishers of men." That means our decision to follow Christ is directly tied in with the responsibility to be an ambassador for Him to a lost and dying world! Following Jesus will cost us everything that the world has to offer. But we count all that as loss, for the surpassing worth of knowing Christ. True followers of Jesus have tasted of the spring of living water found only in Him, and cannot be swayed by the world. To follow Christ is to take up a cross, but it is also to take up fullness of joy. I have seen, I have tasted, I have experienced the infinite worth of Jesus Christ, and in following Him I have received a treasure that cannot be found anywhere else. —*SARAH, AGE 17

2. Why shouldn't we let the sun go down on our wrath?

Why would you be mad at your problems or somebody else when you could be helping people or just having fun? Besides, being mad at anything, animals or humans, just makes us sad and not joyful, and God wants us to be joyful. It also makes you look like a jerk. You don't want to give your problems to others because it will make the situation worse, but talk to others for advice. By the time you go to bed you'll regret you moped at all that day, when you could have been glorifying in His sight!
—Peter, age 13

3. When do you feel judgmental of others?

When I think too highly of myself, I feel like people aren't as good as me. Sometimes I will judge people who look or act different than I do, but then I have to remember that God created all of us as equals and no one is better than anyone else, and we all have our talents and our weaknesses. It doesn't matter how we look or how we act, we are all the same in God's eyes. And sometimes, even though you may not favor someone, you have to accept them just the way they are because God created everyone special and unique in their own way. —Amelia, age 13

4. What is the hardest thing about being a servant?

The hardest part about being a servant to me is when someone is ungrateful. It makes it so much harder to be kind and serve them. —Kinzie, age 15

5. Who in your life has been the best example of a Christlike servant?

I would have to say my grandma! She is constantly praying, and telling me she's praying for me, and it's a major encouragement in my life. She also gets up every morning for quiet time with the Lord. Anytime I feel uneasy, she always knows what to say and leads me to think what Jesus would do. She's a huge example for me in the way of building a relationship with Jesus Christ.
—MELANIE, AGE 16

INTERVIEWS

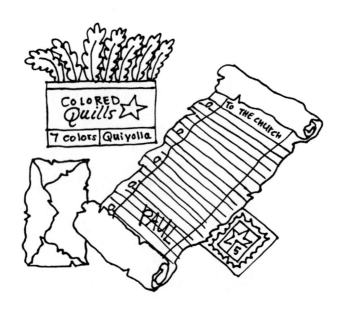

CHAPTER 9
Letters

{ NEW TESTAMENT POSTAL SERVICES }

To God's Holy People in Ephesus:

~ CHRISTIAN LIVING ~

PARAPHRASE OF EPHESIANS 1:1, EPHESIANS 4:17-5:20

This letter is from Paul, chosen by the will of God to be an apostle of Christ Jesus. I am writing to God's holy people in Ephesus, who are faithful followers of Christ Jesus (Ephesians 1:1).

An excerpt from Paul's letter:

So now that you have become a follower of Christ, let's talk about what this means and requires of us. You've all seen how the Gentiles—those who are not children of God—act. They think pointless thoughts, they shut their hearts to learning about God, they grasp things of the world, and they have hearts of greed. They have become desensitized to sin. Is this what a Christian, too, should act like? No, because if not, what separates us as any different from the lost? I'd strongly encourage you to live differently—to set yourself apart from the Gentiles. There's a different way to live.

When you learned about Jesus and His truth, did you learn that you can invite Jesus into your life and go on with your everyday life—the sinful thinking, talking, actions, and such—and it's okay because you've already been forgiven and covered by the blood of Christ? No, you learned that the old man (or woman)—the person you were without Christ—must leave, along with his sinful tendencies, and you must be renewed into a new, clean creation. This new, clean creation is the new and reformed you, *created to be like God—truly righteous and holy* (Ephesians 4:24). This new self should have a new, pure, different way of thinking—a new, pure, different way of living, for that matter. Let's see what we can cover.

For starters, resolve to tell the truth—always. Quit any habit of lying or telling half-truths, and let the new you be honest. After all, Christ never lied, so why should His followers? Also, don't sin or go to sleep when you are angry. Make sure that you have forgiven those you are angry with before the sun sets. Fend off Satan and don't let Him capture your life, as I can assure you he will try to do so.

If you've been stealing, you must stop—instead, put yourself to work and getting your hands into some useful, productive activity. You will not only be saving yourself from breaking the eighth commandment (Exodus 20:15: *You must not steal.*), but you will have a gift through your productivity—something to share with others.

Can you imagine the example that this would set for others if all of us believers aimed with all our hearts to do every one of those concepts I just mentioned? Can you imagine the impression that would make on the Gentiles? There's more, though. When you speak, don't let anything indecent escape your lips. Let your words be pure and meaningful. Make sure that your words encourage others in their walks with Christ, and that everything you say is profitable to the listener. People want to be around those who have good, meaningful things to say. Be conscious that you don't do anything that would hurt the Holy Spirit—this consciousness can keep you from a whole lot of mistakes. As a new creation, there are often times we must go in to the deep, dark, dusty parts of our lives that we have shoved away sins or pushed them aside and do some cleaning. *Get rid of all bitterness, rage, anger, harsh words, and slander, as well as all types of evil behavior* (Ephesians 4:31). That's a lot of cleaning you may have never realized you needed. It's amazing how dirty the old creation looks after we've found something better and cleaner than this world.

Kindness and compassion are key elements in a Christian's behavior towards others. Seldom do you see a Gentile portraying qualities such as these in a genuine, selfless, heartfelt way. Be forgiving—after all, Christ did forgive you. God has set an incredible example for us to follow—and, as His children, love is essential to our new creation's spiritual DNA. We must *walk in love*

(Ephesians 5:2 NIV) as Christ did for us when He gave up His life by dying for us and giving Himself as the sacrifice.

Amidst you all, the believers of Ephesus, there should not be a single indication of anything immoral, impure, or greedy. What kind of message would that send to others about God and His children if we, as believers, were involved in such doings? Same with *obscene stories, foolish talk,* and *coarse jokes* (Ephesians 5:4): for a Christ follower to be engaged in any of these would be inappropriate. We're children of *God!* We would be hypocrites, not practicing what we preach. Do something useful with your mouth, like thanking God. You have so much to be thankful for. *You can be sure that no immoral, impure, or greedy person will inherit the Kingdom of Christ and of God. For a greedy person is an idolater, worshiping the things of this world* (Ephesians 5:5). If any one speaks meaningless words to you, get out of there—fast! God punishes the disobedient, even those who listen to pointless talking. Here's a tip: don't be around those who babble on aimlessly.

Many of us have trouble parting with our old ways and reforming our actions to follow God's instructions on Christian living. But, I will tell you why we must change. Whether it is hard to accept the fact or not, we were living in pitch-black darkness before we entered the light of Jesus Christ. Now that we are in the light, we can see the things we could not see before—such as the wickedness in our lives. We are now *children of light* (Ephesians 5:8 NIV). Just like you won't get bananas from a pear tree, children of light will only give off light! Get to know God. Find out what gratifies the Lord.

The sinful darkness is no place for children of light. Have nothing to do with any dark dealing, deed, or situation, but instead, bring light to the evil, so that it will be found out and put to a stop. It is despicable even to talk about the secret business of the sinners, which is why it is good to expose sin under the light so that the problem can be fixed and pulled up by the root. Everything and everyone put under the light *becomes a light* (Ephesians 5:13 NIV).

So, this being said, watch your lifestyles. Live life wisely, like a Solomon, not unwisely—these are corrupted days, and you have no time to lose. *Make the most of every opportunity* (Ephesians 5:16) to shine your light. Don't live foolishly or get drunk, because indecency is not fit for a follower of Christ. Rather, be full of the Holy Spirit, and speak to the fellow believers in Spirit-inspired *psalms, hymns, and songs* (Ephesians 5:18-19 NIV). As King David did, sing to the Lord and make music to Him straight from your heart. Never stop thanking the Father for everything in Jesus's Name, for He has given you a lot to be thankful for.

The way we live as Christians is so important. We need to stand out—be different from others. Remember, first and foremost, we are representing the Lord our God in everything we do. What kind of impression will we give other people about Jesus? …

Paul

Now what?

If you've ever prayed to Jesus to come live in your heart and be King and Lord of your life, then you have successfully completed Stage One of making the best decision of your life! Now you're ready for Stage Two—the final stage—which requires less talk, more action. Actually, Stage Two really should be just a byproduct of Stage One, considering that once we've committed our life to Christ, we're ready to "...turn from your [our] selfish ways, take up your [our] cross, and follow me [Jesus]" (Matthew 16:24; brackets mine). As the song says, "I have decided to follow Jesus, no turning back..." We have decided, perhaps, but there are still changes and action steps we need to make in order to fully fulfill our duties as "... Christ's ambassadors..." (2 Corinthians 5:20).

I've heard it once said that we should live as though we are Christ's "commercials." What do we make God—Jesus—Christianity—look like? We can see that there are multiple ways to stand out as believers and be children of light. Let's specifically look at ways to reform the way we, as Christians, should handle anger and verbal sins.

SUNSET SETTLING

(AND OTHER CONCEPTS ABOUT ANGER THAT YOU WOULDN'T KNOW UNLESS YOU'VE READ EPHESIANS 4:26-27)

Anger—one of the most powerful, painful, and destructive emotions—is something every single one of us is familiar with. Something or (cough, cough) someone antagonizes us somehow, and then, well, you know how it goes. Our blood slowly heats to a boil. Steam comes out of our ears. Smoke billows from our head. Well, at least, that's what it feels like sometimes. How un-Christian of us to get angry. Or, is it? The Bible actually never tells us that anger in itself is wrong or sinful. In fact, anger is one of the emotions that God displays on several occasions, particularly in the Old Testament when His people were defying His commands. *Wow! Then it's okay to be angry after all!* Well, yes, in a sense, but there's more to it than that.

Although God would get very angry with His people, you have to understand that His people were truly testing His authority—they were running away from His commands. Finally, God hit His limit—which was a very high limit indeed, as we know from Psalm 103:8 that, "The Lord is compassionate and merciful, *slow to get angry* and filled with unfailing love" (italics mine). He is slow to anger—and the Israelites managed to make God's anger-o-meter slowly boil to the maximum level. He had good reasons!

Let's be honest with ourselves—we've all been angry without good reasons before. We were mad at Garris for talking to *our* friend. We were mad at Tara for not buying us a Dr. Pepper from the vending machine when we didn't have any money and she had enough for five sodas. We were mad at Roy for coming in first place in the competition—leaving us in second place. Remember how in the Sermon on the Mount, Jesus states that anyone who is angry at someone without a cause is a murderer? It's not a good idea to get worked up over trifling, paltry matters. Not only is excessive anger physically unhealthy for our body, but someone who gets mad easily is going to be an object of avoidance to friends and family. I mean, would you dare make a move around a person that was just going to get upset at you for every little thing you did that displeased them? Ephesians 4:26-27 outlines some regulations for us to keep anger under control:

- …*don't sin by letting anger control you*…
- …*Don't let the sun go down while you are still angry*…
- …*do not give the devil a foothold* (NIV).

Paul knew that Christians get angry. He got angry. Don't believe it? Read Acts 15:36-41, where Paul and Barnabas go their own separate ways after some friction between them. It is pretty obvious that they were mad at each other. When we feel anger burning

THE GREATEST BOOK YOU'VE NEVER READ

within us, we should consciously get control of our emotions—fast—and be careful to not sin. It is very easy to just let the passion in the anger loose and cause all sorts of damage and destruction.

You are probably very familiar with the "heat of the moment," when people say, do, and feel things about others that they don't really mean—it's also the time when a person's true colors come out.You might hang around Elsie and her brother Freddy every week, and they always seem to get along great. Then, the day rolls around that Freddy accidentally spills paint on her new shoes, and she hollers names at her brother that you wouldn't dare utter. She may have been understandably angry, but she's putting a lot at jeopardy (i.e., her relationships, reputation, etc.) and causing damage (hurting her brother, hurting her relationship/reputation with you) by lashing out uncontrollably. It's best to learn this concept at as early an age as possible, because some people go through their whole lives letting anger control them and rule their lives, destroying themselves and those around them. Chances are, you probably know someone who has lived a broken life due to anger issues. Even in the "heat of the moment," run from sin. In fact, fight the flesh and do the opposite of your angry feelings.

Now, for the next one: going to sleep angry. Doesn't sound terribly bad, right? When we let anger sit, it soon spoils into bitterness, whether we realize it or not. Ten years down the road, even after Tom spread a false rumor about us, we're still going to wonder why we have this callused, hurt spot in our hearts. We can't brush our anger under the carpet. We have to stare it in the eye, face-to-face, and release it, apply forgiveness where necessary, and forget it. After all, love "…keeps no record of being wronged" (1 Corinthians 13:5).

Don't let your head hit the pillow without clearing yourself of any anger or unfinished forgiveness. You'll never regret it.

Last, but definitely not least: no giving the devil a foothold! What, exactly, does that mean? It means that, when the devil comes a-knocking at your heart's door—which he will—you give him a blow he'll never forget. You kick him off God's property. You pull out "...the sword of the Spirit, which is the word of God," (Ephesians 6:17) and you fight him and defeat him—no way will you let him set foot within your life. Resisting his foothold means shouting, "Get out of here, Satan, in the name of Jesus!" and calling Psalm 9:11 (NIV): "Sing praises to the Lord who reigns in Jerusalem. Tell the world about his unforgettable deeds." When the devil tries to tempt us into being angry at nothing, or when he tries to get us to sin in anger or not settle matters before the sun sets, we speak the Word of God and praise the Lord, because, as believers, our focus is on Jesus! We remove ourselves as fast as we can from temptation. Take in a deep breath, leave the room for a second if you must, hold your tongue until you're ready to make things right, and, since we love the Lord, obey His commands (John 14:15).

However, anger can, in fact, be a righteous feeling. *Righteous anger? Sounds like an oxymoron.* Well, what about when people truly get treated unfairly? What about big issues, such as abortion? What about when someone blasphemes (uses in vain; uses disrespectfully as a curse word) the Lord's name or talks bad about Him? There are plenty of cases in which anger is, undoubtedly, justified and proper. Think about how even Jesus overturned the money tables in the Temple in His anger (Matthew 21:12-13)! Yet, we still must, even in righteous anger, apply the three regulations Paul lists, because anger is an unruly beast that must be watched closely.

ZANE TOLD POLLY WHO TOLD ANDREW WHO TOLD CLARA...
(EPHESIANS 4:29,31, 5:4,6-7)

"Psshhh... only girly girls gossip!" "Gossiping? Who, me? No, I was giving a prayer request!" "I was just informing them... er, getting informed!" "Well, I only tell those kinds of things to my trustworthy friend who can keep a secret!" Don't fall into any of the lies about gossip—it never did anybody any good! Everybody hates gossip, yet they love it too much to give it up! Gossip is a horrible, appalling sin when it's about us, but when we're the ones engaging in it, it is just about the juiciest, most engrossing topic in the world. And sometimes, at the time we're gossiping, it really doesn't feel like a sin... and it's hard to stop.

By gossip, I am referring to what Paul called "slander": when you make someone look bad while talking about them with someone else. The worst part about gossip is that it's a virus. Say you meet Gerald, and he seems like a nice guy. The next week, you see Gerald again. Chances are, gossiping about Gerald had never even crossed your mind that week. You had nothing bad to say about him because he had given you nothing bad to think about him. Makes sense, right? So when you see him for the second time, conversation starts out as usual and you are getting to know him a little better. You are talking about basketball, when all of a sudden, Gerald says, "Oh, yeah! There's this one guy on my team—I don't even know how he made it on, he's so horrible. In my opinion, he's best at bench warming!" In that instant, Gerald verbally handed you the ticket, or should I say, license, to go and gossip about him with justification. But then, you gossip to Phoebe about Gerald, and then Phoebe now has the gossip license for you. See how it works? Similar to a lie, it's a cycle that snowballs out of control.

Gossip isn't the only deadly sin of the tongue that Paul warns us from falling into, nor is it the only time that verbal sins are mentioned in this section of Scripture: there's "...foul or abusive language..." (Ephesians 4:29), "...harsh words, and slander..." (Ephesians 4:31), "...obscene stories, foolish talk, and coarse jokes..." (Ephesians 5:4), and, "...empty words..." (Ephesians 5:6 NIV). It all boils down to verbal sins, really.

Ephesians 4:29 (NIV) says, "Do not let any unwholesome talk come out of your mouths, but only what is helpful for building others up according to their needs, that it may benefit those who listen." It seems that half the words that leave people's lips nowadays serve no beneficial purpose, if any, which brings up another verse: "Let no one deceive you with empty words, for because of such things God's wrath comes on those who are disobedient. Therefore do not be partners with them" (Ephesians 5:6-7 NIV). All of the speech sins mentioned in Paul's discourse on Christian living can fall under unwholesome talk, but what is the problem with empty talk?

We've all heard the phrase, "If you can't say anything nice, don't say anything at all." The Book of Proverbs covers the subject of holding your tongue well. You may have heard Solomon's Proverbs 17:28 before, which says, "Even fools are thought wise when they keep silent; with their mouths shut, they seem intelligent."

I couldn't have put it better myself. When we ramble on about nonsense or try to make up stuff to say, we can end up saying hurtful, inappropriate, or rude things unintentionally. A lot of times, empty words happen when someone is trying to be funny, concoct a comeback, or show-off. As my dad would say, "Don't let your motor run." If our mouth is spitting out word after word after word on an aimless mission to get to nowhere, that spells trouble. We not only expose our lack of knowledge on a subject and maturity deficiency, but it looks bad for a Christ follower to be idly spewing out random, thoughtless remarks, which have a tendency to end up as bad comments.

And, of course, there's the all-too-familiar trap of "Obscene stories, foolish talk, and coarse jokes..." (Ephesians 5:4) that Paul warns us of. Sometimes, we find ourselves surrounded with the perfect audience for an off-color comment or joke—we could have instant friends if we just make the crowd laugh. Before making that joke, let's evaluate: will *everybody* think it's funny? Let's see— Karley, yes; Hayden, check; Silvia, yup; God—ye... what? Oh yeah. God is standing there, too—and He doesn't think coarse joking is funny. Obscenity and the like are as common as houseflies in our desensitized generation. Walk down the halls of any school or enter any movie theater and hear at least a word or two that would have caused any mother from the 1950's to stick a bar of soap in her child's mouth for a year. In Matthew 12:36, Jesus says, "And I tell you this, you must give an account on judgment day for every idle word you speak." Unless we want to explain ourselves for that ugly remark or that euphemism, dirty talking and joking isn't in our best interest.

NEW TESTAMENT POSTAL SERVICES:
To the Scattered Twelve Tribes:
~ THE TONGUE ~

PARAPHRASE OF JAMES 1:1, JAMES 3:2-12

This letter is from James, a slave of God and of the Lord Jesus Christ. I am writing to the "twelve tribes"—Jewish believers scattered abroad. Greetings! (James 1:1).

An excerpt from James's letter:

We all have our struggles and stumbles. The person who can control his or her tongue is perfect—one that can easily control their entire body.

Just like people put bits in horses' mouths to get them to turn whichever way they choose, and ships have rudders that determine the course of their path, the body follows whichever way the tongue leads. The rudder of a ship is so small, yet it can turn a massive vessel to the east or to the west, despite the interference of powerful winds. See the tongue—that small pink member of your body—but look at the things it can say! A little spark can cause a roaring fire that burns down a forest. The tongue is a flame—an evil little part of every human's mouth that possesses full capability to ruin a person's life with sin and send the person to hell by the words it says.

Mankind has successfully been able to tame dogs, horses, birds, dolphins, and the like—but they will never be able to tame the tongue, an unruly beast with no boss.

The tongue never takes a break from evil—it is a container of deadly venom. It is a two-faced double-crosser—look at how that same pink little muscle both gives praise to the Lord and curses others, who, by the way, are the Lord's creations, made in His Image. This is terribly wrong! Do saltwater springs give both salty water and fresh water? Or do freshwater springs alternate between both fresh and saltwater? No! What about figs, do they grow on grape vines, or the other way around? I didn't think so…

James

Weren't We Just Talking About Words?

Yes. We were. The power of the tongue is such an important subject—not to mention, especially among people (yeah, even Christians) today, it is such a disregarded subject. Sometimes I've thought, *Words are just different vibrations of vocal chords with our tongue and lips moving to form different sequences of sounds…*

How is it, then, that words can have such power and importance? Words say what we're thinking. Have you noticed the power words have? God created the universe with words in Genesis 1. God cursed serpents and mankind in Genesis 3. Esau gave up his privileged first-born blessings for a bowl of lentil stew with his rash words in Genesis 25:29-34. Jephthah made a hasty vow on the spur of the moment which cost him the life of his only daughter in Judges 11:29-40. Jesus said, "Be healed!" to the leper in Matthew 8:3, "And instantly the leprosy disappeared." Ananias and Sapphira died because of words in Acts 5:1-10. Jesus forgave people with words. Jesus and the apostles performed miracles through words. That's enough evidence to prove that yes, words are a huge deal!

Did you see how James said that anyone able to control the tongue is a perfect person? A perfect person! Which means, you guessed it, nobody can fully control the tongue. The tongue is the driving force of our whole life! Our tongue can ruin our lives—or, it can build our lives upwards. The tongue can sing songs of praise to the Lord on Sunday morning, and it can spit insults at a friend on Monday. The tongue is a menacing beast. What, then, can be done about this verbal dilemma?

Thankfully, God sent Jesus to take on all our sins and die for us so that we wouldn't have to. We don't have to be completely perfect to enter His Kingdom anymore, because there is grace that covers us. We must have the perfect Son of God, Jesus, living in our hearts to enter. However, we know from Mark 10:27 that, "…Humanly speaking, it is impossible. But not with God. Everything is possible with God." *So the impossible task of taming the tongue can, in fact, be accomplished?* You heard correctly, my friend. And we don't even need to call in animal control, wildlife rescue, or the SWAT team for help!

The Little Rudder That Could

I like Paul's analogies with the rudder of the boat and the bit of the horse. Both of those small little pieces of machinery lead the vessel whichever way the captain or rider decides to turn it. We can use our tongues to build others up, praise the Lord, and help ourselves. Yet, our tongue is also fully capable of ruining our relationships, causing deep wounds and scars, and digging a pit for us to fall into. Well, how do you like that—we are in danger of our very own tongues!

Listen to the truth in James 3:6: "And the tongue is a flame of fire. It is a whole world of wickedness, corrupting your entire body. It can set your whole life on fire, for it is set on fire by hell itself." Whether it's through gossip, slander, insults, ignorance, dirty joking, dirty talking, cussing, swearing, cursing, rudeness—you name it—the tongue knows its capabilities, sometimes even before we do.

Even at the young age of about three or four, my sister Genevieve had invented her own bad word—"boochie"—that she used whenever she didn't get her way. She didn't like the way I played stuffed animals with her? *Boochie!* She didn't like that Mommy wouldn't let her get up from the table until she'd finished her food? *Boochie!* The sinful nature, even of a young child, proves itself relentless time and time again. About ten years after Genevieve's "boochie"-yelling years, the fourth sister in the lineup, three-year-old Harmony (who, by the way, was never told about "boochie"), invented her own angry word—"poochie!" *Boochie?! Poochie?!* Hmmm... this can't be coincidence. Right from the start, we humans instinctively resort to sin, including that of the tongue, no matter how innocent and cute the sin starts out to be.

The key to taming the "yapparatus" in your mouth is self-control—the last (but not least) fruit of the Spirit mentioned in Galatians 5:22-23; not to mention, one of the character traits that I have not yet heard someone name their child! True self-control is impossible without Christ and God's Holy Spirit living and working through us. The Holy Spirit is the one that gives us self-control. One of my favorite Proverbs is 25:28, "A person without self-control is like a city with broken-down walls." This fruit of the Spirit is a core food for the spiritual being of a Christian. Without it, we have no defense against evil. We're vulnerable to Satan's attacks. The non-Christian concept of "will power" just does not work as long, as well, and sometimes, at all, as self-control does.

Recipe for Trouble

Ingredients: someone with a sinful human nature, a tongue, a brain, listeners, and a moment to speak. Directions: Put sinful natured human with tongue and brain inside a room with none or more listeners and give a moment to speak. Watch disaster take place. Takes approximately no time at all.

Why does opening the mouth have to be so disastrous? Well, the fact is, it doesn't have to be. The problem, however, is that few people have mastered the art of filtering their words, thinking before they speak, and knowing when to remain silent. If I recall correctly, the Book of Proverbs had some good nuggets of wisdom on that subject. Remember Proverbs 17:28 from earlier in this chapter? I find it amazing that a foolish person can appear wise simply by remaining silent! Here's an age-old rule of thumb: If you don't have anything to say, just don't say anything, 'cause even fools who know when to hold their tongue look like wise people!

We can probably all agree that saying that it feels nice to have the last word in an argument is an understatement. When our opponent keeps throwing logs on the fire, provoking a reaction out of us, our main focus becomes true *justice*…true justice being that we win the argument. This tendency is due to our pride. What we don't usually take into account for is that the person we're arguing with may have just as much pride, fight (and fantastically original comebacks like, "I know you are, but what am *I?!*"), and passion for "justice" as we do. There are some people out there—maybe even you—that are verbal gladiators—they will "fight to the death" in an argument without a moment of rest until they win. I've been there, done that. Y'know what? As painful as it is to even think of giving up such a victory, it's not that big of a deal. Just let the other person win. Remain silent. We can't get ourselves into trouble with our words unless we speak. So, when in doubt, just don't.

THE TONGUE AND THE HEART: A SECRET ALLIANCE

Most likely, you can empathize with the feeling of thinking you knew someone well, then you find out that they aren't at all the good, godly person you thought they were. Well, I sure hate to break it to you, but… there's something very close to you (and I mean *close*) that is a menacing, two-faced creature. Wait for it, wait for it… it's—it's your tongue. Yes, you heard correctly—your tongue. But did you know that your tongue is simply your heart's field agent doing the dirty work for it? That's right—the same tongue that sang *Amazing Grace* and *Holy Is the Lord* last Sunday and later led the youth group in prayer for the orphans in Uganda just dropped a verbal bomb on its sister!

James 3:9-12 says, "Sometimes it praises our Lord and Father, and sometimes it curses those who have been made in the image of God. And so blessing and cursing come pouring out of the same mouth. Surely, my brothers and sisters, this is not right! Does a spring of water bubble out with both fresh water and bitter water? Does a fig tree produce olives, or a grapevine produce figs? No, and you can't draw fresh water from a salty spring." As God's children, we should train our tongues to be honest to our beliefs. So, unless we truly believe in insulting others (which children of God should not), our tongue should be constantly bring glory and praise to God. It's good to check ourselves on that. *Was that remark I just made to my friend honoring to God? Were the words that just left my mouth "an encouragement to those who hear[d] them? (Ephesians 4:29; brackets mine)"*

To be completely honest with you, I have trouble with this one sometimes. Especially during family conversations, time and time again I'll go digging for negative things to say, searching high and low for a cynical or sarcastic remark to make. That beast of a tongue does not like it when I pull back the reins on it—it does not want to be tamed. And guess what—that's wrong. That's two-faced. That's the fig tree giving olives. Our family life is our real life—who we are around our family is *who we really are*. That's our real person. A lot of times, it is much easier to say God-honoring, God-praising things when we're around our friends. We want to impress them and make them like us and think highly of us. But our family—well, that's just our family. You know, the people God hand-chose as our learning and living environment to strengthen

203

one another and to expand His Kingdom as a powerful force together. Just them. That's often how we look at it, and we go and live the secret life of the tongue once again. As children of God, we should… wait, no—you finish the sentence. You know this stuff. Need a hint? Read James 3:9-12 and Ephesians 4:29.

I love getting letters. Letter writing is sort of a lost, "old-fashioned" art that I've picked up as a hobby in the past few years. Back in Paul and James's day, letter writing was *the* source of communication. In order to tell the church in a certain city God's latest revelation to him, or to scold a certain church for some shortcomings, Paul wrote letters of all shapes, matters, and sizes to get his message safely delivered. If you remember from the very beginning of the book, God wrote you and me a letter too. A letter with sixty-six books enclosed. It is a message of love, hope, glory, correction, encouragement, and salvation. It's the Bible. Go ahead, tear open the envelope, put out the letter, and enjoy God's notes to *you*.

I DARE YOU...

Anger is a destructive, life-crushing emotion. Families, marriages, churches, and friendships are ripped apart at the seams when this emotion is not properly dealt with. Find out from your parents, grandparents, or another godly Christian adult about someone whose life became a mess due to anger. I can think of a story right of the top of my head that my parents shared with me. Discuss the points that you can learn from the situation. What could have prevented that person's life from crashing down so hard? How can you avoid making the same mistakes in your life?

We've all "put our foot in our mouth" as the old (and insanitary) saying goes. Learn to use self-control in everything you do, of course, but focus on your speech. Maybe hook up with an accountability partner (with the usual characteristics of godly, Christian, trustworthy, etc, etc. Maybe even a family member!) to talk with every week or so, and both of you can discuss how you did on "praising the Lord" in all that you said to everyone you spoke with that week. Usually, having someone monitoring you in a certain part of your life will make you more careful with what you do. Try out verbal accountability for a while.

FOOD FOR THOUGHT...

1. When is it hardest for you to control your anger?

When I'm not walking in the Spirit and I haven't done my devotions (aka spent time with the Lord), it is easy to be in the flesh and want to fight back when something makes me mad. —DANIEL, AGE 12

2. As God's Own children, why shouldn't we slander?

We shouldn't slander because if we are going to demonstrate God's love for us, His sons and daughters, we shouldn't belittle other people just to make ourselves feel better or get what we want. If we are going to be God's love, the very core of who He is and how He cares about us, we must not be mean to others just because they don't share the same beliefs as us. Why waste your time hurting others when you could be sharing His love? Like it says in Proverbs 15:30 (NKJV), "The light of the eyes rejoices the heart, And a good report makes the bones healthy." *And another passage a few verses over confirms it:* "Pleasant words are like a honeycomb, Sweetness to the soul and health to the bones" *(Proverbs 16:24 NKJV).* —ELIZABETH, AGE 15

3. When is it hardest for you to show self-control in your speech?

When I'm angry with someone.—Sydney, age 16

4. Why should we, as believers, "watch our tongue?"

We as believers are image bearers of Christ. That means we are called to be like Christ (Eph. 5:1-2, 1 John 2:6). What is Christ's image that we are called to walk according to? Love one another. This is part of the greatest commandment that Jesus gave us (Matt. 22:36-40). If we, as believers, were to talk to people around us in a disrespectful, un-loving way, how would that be showing them the love of Christ? Therefore, we should all "watch our tongue" as a way to show His tremendous love to the world, by showing others the respect of speaking to them in a way that would make them feel loved. —Meriel, age 17

5. What response should we, as God's own sons and daughters, have towards others who do not control their tongues?

First of all, don't let their words cause you to be offended and quickly forgive them. If they are talking about someone else, ask them how they would feel if someone said that about them. Politely walk off if the conversation doesn't turn positive. —Madelyn, age 9

CHAPTER 10
The Why

You've Seen the Previews...

You've seen a prisoner get shipwrecked and survive a deadly viper bite without so much as a sickly symptom. You've seen a follower betray his master for a gruesome Roman death. You've seen a young widow meet her match, a monstrous fish vomit up a fugitive prophet, the future dwelling place of Christians, and you've heard the inside scoop from famous disciples and apostles. Hopefully you've discovered that the Bible isn't all thees and thous of religious text just for the old times clergy. The Bible is for us! God's Book is for you and me!

But why should we want to read the Bible every single day? What's the difference whether we do or don't read the Word daily? Wouldn't reading it every Sunday during church suffice? Wouldn't skimming a verse now and then be enough to check that task off of our checklist? The answer is no. Reading the Bible should not be a chore at all. You know what God wants? He wants our hearts. He wants to make us love Him and want Him with all of our hearts. By reading God's Word, we get a glimpse at the very heart of God, the very words He and His Son spoke, the very history He orchestrated, and so on and so forth. God's Book wasn't written to be the bestseller at the Christian book stores, to be a vintage leather decoration crowning the table, nor to be chore number eleven on our to-do list, right after we pick up our room. It was written to change hearts and to draw you and I closer to God.

Every single book of the Bible, from Genesis to Revelation, is in there for a purpose. I can't say that I understand why each one is in there, but God knows. For every person's situation, lifestyle, sins, and heart, there is something in the Bible to address it. God was thorough when planning out the Bible.

Yes, That's the Book for Me

We talked a little bit about the Bible and its many "properties," you could say, at the beginning of the book. Let's take a quick review of the old and introduce some of the new! The Bible is:

- A great piece of literature in itself
- An encyclopedia on all things love
- Our field guide to life
- Our life manual
- A insightful scientific record
- A shockingly accurate historical document
- God's Own Words
- One of the ways God talks to us

- As King David said, "…a lamp to guide my feet and a light for my path" (Psalm 119:105).
- A handbook we should be reading *daily!*

The Bible, as you will remember, is for everybody. It's for City Cindy, Farmer Franklin, Young Yolanda, Old Octavius, Talkative Tanya, Quiet Quinton, Mathematic Matthew, Grammar Gretel, Tidy Timothy, Wild Wendy, Outgoing Oscar, and Shy Sheila, to name a few. No matter who you are and what you've done, God is ready to speak some really great things to you through His Word and to draw you in. You could be Angelic Arty, Good Gwendolyn, Perfect Patty, Pure Percival, or Sweet Sarah—or, you could be Rotten Rita, Wicked Wilbur, Sinful Sophia, Bad Brock, or Evil Eddie (okay, I'm having too much fun with this!). *Whoever* you are—the Bible is not for you to ignore!

Obedient Oliver

Okay, okay! That was the last one! I promise! Now, to talk about obedience.

Did you know that reading the Bible comes with rewards? Well, if you've never read the Bible, you probably wouldn't know… because it says so, right in the Bible! "…blessed are all who hear the word of God and put it into practice" (Luke 11:28). Did you catch the last part? I guess just reading the Bible doesn't help. We're supposed to put it into practice through obedience. The Book of Psalms goes on and on about the Law of the Lord and its greatness, and how we are so blessed to be corrected by the Lord.

Listen to the kind of praise that King David would give the Lord about His Word: "For the word of the Lord holds true, and we can trust everything he does" (Psalm 33:4). David even praised God for His Commandments and His correction: "Joyful are those you discipline, Lord, those you teach with your instructions,"(Psalm 94:12); "Oh, how I love your law! I meditate on it all day long" (Psalm 119:97 NIV). The Lord's Law was truly King David's joy!

When you were little, did you ever tell your parents that you were so grateful that they punished you, and did you ever express how much you loved their rules? Neither did I. But, a few years down the road, when their rules had kept me from getting hit by a car, getting electrocuted, and all sorts of other hurtful possibilities, I really am thankful. I'm also thankful for the more recent rules that have kept me from other dangers, such as getting hit by the fast-moving media bandwagons, like the wrong kinds of music, role-models, movies, books, friends, websites, and so on. I mean, just *think* of where our world would be without rules! Rules rule! If our society didn't have any form of written law available to follow, then everything would be disastrous—car wrecks, crime, and all kinds of messiness. When you think about it, while one can be a "law abiding citizen" on this earth with some idea of right and wrong, there really are no absolute standards or morals unless someone sets a firm line between good and evil.

God's Law shows us what guilty sinners we are by nature. As Romans 3:20 says, "…The law simply shows us how sinful we are." Mention even a few of His commandments—do not steal, do not use God's Name in vain—and we can tell all too quickly that we have broken His commandments on numerous occasions… like, everyday. Then, we realize our need for a Savior. But don't let me give away chapter 12 just yet!

Some people have had bad experiences with rules and regulations. Sometimes, when people get fed up with the rules and regulations set by their parents, authorities, or churches, they rebel and their hearts turn hard as rock towards such rules. Let this be clear: God is not trying to make our lives miserable. He is not trying to keep us from having fun. He gave us rules in our best interest! He gave them to us for our protection.

Sometimes, parents will set rules that their child doesn't understand or doesn't agree with, and then they decide to sprint in the opposite direction. Just like this rebelling child, sometimes we, as people with a nature that tries to revolt against God, run from His commands.

Some of us are just more prone to be rule-followers, while some of us tend to want to test the rules… to find out that we are wrong…

to try things our way for a while… even to rebel. For me, it honestly depends on the rule. For instance, with a rule like, "Keep your eyes on the road when driving," I don't debate it and find it easy to follow. But, on rules like, "Don't boss around your sister," I usually "make exceptions." And, on days when I'm told that I can only eat *two donuts* when we go to Krispy Kreme, I find it *extremely* hard not to rebel!

Do you want to know what God's Word says about rebellion? It's kind of shocking. 1 Samuel 15:23: "Rebellion is as sinful as witchcraft…" Yikes! God passionately hates witchcraft. It's an absolutely forbidden practice. And He's comparing *rebellion* to witchcraft? It must be a huge deal! So, to rebel against God and His Word is never a good idea.

So, if this were a focus group, we'd probably all be nodding our heads in agreement that, yes, rules are good. We could never even begin to live up to God's commands if it weren't for Jesus living in our hearts (if you have accepted Him, that is) and for the Holy Spirit in us. Thankfully, the Bible sets a standard for our lives, and it gives us the ultimate role model—Jesus! We now have the knowledge and desire to do what He asks of us every moment. In a nutshell: the Bible shows us God's commandments and teaches us how to obey them. It's as simple as that. When we spend time reading God's Word every single day, we are reminded that He makes the rules and that we'd better obey them, for our sake and for His.

Hello My Name Is I Am

God already knows you, but do you know Him (chapter 12 will explain how you, too, can know Him if you don't already)? Through reading the Bible daily, you will continue to explore His personality as one God, three Persons—the Trinity—God the Father, the Son, and the Holy Spirit. Think about the awesome opportunity we have to actually personally *know*—not just meet and greet, shake hands with, have a brief lunch with, or get acquainted with—the Creator of the Universe, the Author of the Bible and of History, the Orchestrator of Time, the Redeemer, the God of All, the Great I Am (Exodus 3:14)! He gets to be our Friend and we get to be His friend! Life doesn't get more exciting than that!

Have you ever seen someone newly in love? How does that person behave? They're kind of in their own world of elation. They talk about the person of their affections, talk with them, contact them, read messages from them, ask mutual friends about them… (Etc., etc.) You get the idea. To put it colloquially, they're crazy about them! Matthew 6:21 says, "Wherever your treasure is, there the desires of your heart will also be." As the church, we are the bride of Christ (2 Corinthians 11:2)—er, fiancé, technically. We will be His bride one day. I wonder to myself, *Am I so in love with my Savior that He is my only desire? Am I so excited about Jesus's tremendous love for me that I can't help but share the good news? Am I simply overflowing with His joy that I long to read and memorize His Words so I can have them hidden in my heart* (Psalm 119:11)? To sum it up, our relationship with God can be described like this: "I am my beloved's and my beloved is mine…" (Song of Solomon 6:3 NIV).

Reading the Bible each day is like reading the Love Letter that God has written to us. We don't just want to read it once and put it away forever. We want to read it again and again and again! We want to read it to others. We want to ponder each word and memorize each stanza. If we skip a day from reading it, we suffer from the effects of withdrawal. His Letter is our most prized possession!

Ready or Not, Here We Come!

As you will remember, if you have Jesus in your heart, you are Christ's ambassador (2 Corinthians 5:20)! You and I have such a high honor to be working under such a Great Boss! Ambassadors possess the job of representing their country in foreign lands. As ambassadors for Christ, we represent Him and His Kingdom in this world, which is not our final home (we are not of this world—John 15:19).

As King David said in Psalm 119:19 (NIV), "I am a stranger on earth; do not hide your commands from me." As strangers on this earth, we should be aware of the fact that we will run into a lot of natives to the earth—those in the bondage of Satan's clutches. Let me tell you a well-kept secret: Satan doesn't want you to be a Christian. He really doesn't. He hates Christians. He hates non-Christians. But he especially hates and targets the faith of Christians because he hates our Master—God. So, what is he going to do about it? He's going to try to trip us up with his obstacles and throw our faith off by shooting his flaming darts and keeping us from fully knowing what our inheritance in Jesus is. He's going to try to get us to believe the lies that he subtly whispers in our minds and ears. He'll put them on movies and TV shows. He'll stick some in the mouths of some people around us. He'll fill the mouths of professors and schoolteachers with them. He'll go to the ends of the earth to get us to stop loving God, mess up a pure and truthful worldview, and fall away from our faith. Are we going to let him win? *No way.*

By reading the Holy Word of God, we become informed. We become educated in the pure, unblemished, truth, and it ultimately becomes engraved in our hearts and minds. Satan tries to suck us into his world of false wisdom. He wants us to forget the simplicity of the gospel and of Jesus. In these situations, we remind ourselves of what His Book of Truth says. What do we do when someone challenges our beliefs? We stand our ground. We plant ourselves upon His Holy Word. The Lord used His servants to write His very words. The Bible is truth (John 17:17, Revelation 22:6)! See what the Bible has to say about soupy worldviews, messy philosophies, and twisted theologies, and read 1 Corinthians 1:18-29 for encouragement and clarity.

What I'm getting at here is, when we read the Bible daily, it's like we're loading up on ammunition to fire at the enemy. We are becoming more and more equipped to defend our faith, not only to keep our own feet stable, but to be able to draw others to the beauty of the gospel and of Christianity! When our lives reflect what we read, we become a living, breathing, moving, walking testimony for believers and nonbelievers alike. You see, if we don't read the Bible and head out into the world to do our job as ambassadors, we are like skydivers jumping out of a plane without a parachute, or a bee farmer collecting honey from the hives without the special netted suit (I love that analogy... particularly because I just came up with it and it actually works!).

I'm so thankful that the Lord didn't drop us on this earth with a mission and leave us without instructions! He left us a big Instruction Book to train us, direct us, challenge us, correct us, equip us, and strengthen us. By reading the Bible every day, we are filling ourselves with knowledge and wisdom, whether we realize it at first or not. We are equipping ourselves to be mighty for the Lord. We are covering ourselves with the armor of God (Ephesians 6:10-17).

PLEASE LEAVE YOUR MESSAGE AFTER THE VERSE

I've fallen for some pretty clever voicemails before. I've had friends set their recording as a conversation, and of course, I go along talking (yet highly confused) until the beep, and I then realize I've been tricked. Thankfully, God keeps His messages simple—without losing any of the power within them. Not only that, but we never get His voicemail. He's always listening to us. Now, let's ask the question again: Why should we read the Bible daily? Because our Savior is trying to talk to us through the main line. He wants us to pick up the Book He's given us, because He's talking to us and He doesn't want us to miss the incredible Words He has to say to us.

The Bible is like our form of mail from God—His Letter! Sometimes I've wondered what it would be like to pick up the Bible as long and as often as I would pick up an electronic device to play with or correspond with friends. For instance, as often as I check my blog stats or email or texts, what if I was picking up my Bible and checking God's messages to me?

We briefly touched on the subject of the "still, small voice" that God can speak to us in. Sometimes, the still, small voice speaks by a verse jumping off the page at us. Maybe we're struggling with something and looking for answers, when all of a sudden, you read a verse that spot-on fits your situation. I sure feel a flood of encouragement when that happens to me. Think about it this way: Of all the thousands of verses in the Bible you could've read, you read that one—the perfect Words that spoke straight to your heart. God really has a way with communication.

That still, small voice is the Holy Spirit inclining you towards or away from something. This "Holy Spirit alarm" warns you when something is not right or when you should do something by using a still, small voice only your heart can hear. But, without reading the Bible, how will we learn how to be attentive to the Spirit or how to listen with our heart? By reading the Bible everyday, we learn how to listen to the still, small voice and to the directions of the Holy Spirit.

The Lord will sometimes use authorities or influences in our life to speak to us. He might use your parents, pastors/youth pastors, mentors, or sometimes friends. Whoever the Lord chooses to speak to us through, we must follow the example of the people of Berea in the book of Acts. Acts 17:11 (NIV) says: "Now the Berean Jews were of more noble character than those in Thessalonica, for they received the message with great eagerness and examined the Scriptures every day to see if what Paul said was true." God's Words will agree with the Bible. If something you hear seems off and it is not in harmony with the Scriptures, chances are it is not from the Lord.

Really, God can speak to us through anyone and anything—if you've ever read Numbers 22:21-39, you know that God has even used *animals* to deliver His messages, such as a donkey speaking to Balaam. I'm not saying that God is planning on speaking to us through Rover or Fluffy, but what I am saying is that we should never put limit God's power and actions. When He has a message for us (which He always does), He finds a way to get it to us—our part is to be attentive, aware of His Presence, and listen. Sometimes this means pressing the brakes on our go-go-go mindset and taking five minutes of silence, really focusing on the Lord and listening to Him. If we aren't reading the Bible everyday—because His Word is one of the main ways that He *will* indeed speak to us—are we being very good listeners? No one likes to talk to an audience that isn't listening.

I want to hear God's Own Words for myself everyday. I know He has great, personalized things to say to me because He created me and knows me from the inside out. He knows every facet of my being and every area in my life. He knows every sin I've committed, every act of kindness I've ever performed, every thought that's ever crossed my mind, every word I've ever said, every affection, dislike, and every emotion I've ever felt. He knows exactly where He has for me to go in life and how to get me there. He can speak powerful, darkness-penetrating Words that can soften any hardness on my heart and transform me on the spot. That is why I want to listen to His mighty, deep, loving Words. He knows you in that way also, and He wants to do the same for you, too.

ENCOURAGEMENT FUEL STATION— FREE PER GALLON

The truth is, life isn't always good (despite what the *Life is Good* t-shirts might say). Sometimes we can really be disheartened in our Christian walk. Sometimes, we can start wondering, "Why am I doing this? Life is hard!" Sometimes, we wonder how well we are doing being servants of Christ. Sometimes, we need someone to give us security and to assure us that everything will be alright.

The Bible is Encouragement Central—it's like a gas station for believers to come and fill up their tanks with God's joyous truths about themselves. God loves to tell us all about what we are capable of doing for Him, what He has in store for us, and what character traits He finds praiseworthy. If you've grown up in church, you've probably heard of the "Fruits of the Spirit" put to the tune of a song sometime in your elementary school years. Can you name all nine? *Love, joy, peace, patience, kindness, goodness, faithfulness, gentleness, and self-control.*

The question is not, "What kind of encouragement can we draw from the Bible?" Because, seriously, what kind of encouragement *can't* we draw from the Bible? God knows every heart and every situation—and every corresponding nugget of hope to hearten us, strengthen us, and encourage us. It doesn't take too much searching to stumble upon one of God's precious Words of encouragement.

For instance, God's Word says in 1 Corinthians 10:13, "The temptations in your life are no different from what others experience.

And God is faithful. He will not allow the temptation to be more than you can stand. When you are tempted, he will show you a way out so that you can endure." Now don't tell me that verse isn't bursting at the seams with encouraging! Paul, the "model" Christian, was assuring us that the struggles, challenges, and temptations that we go through are not abnormal; rather, others are going through the same things as we are. We're not alone fighting a new, unfamiliar enemy never known to humans before. There are others out there going through the exact same struggles. And we won't be tempted with more than we can withstand. Every time we face a temptation, He's also provided an escape route—a way out of it. I love that verse, don't you?

What about Proverbs 3:5-6: "Trust in the Lord with all your heart; do not depend on your own understanding. Seek his will in all you do, and he will show you which path to take." We have a command to put our full trust in the Lord's hands, surrendering them completely so that we are no longer the ones in control, and seeking His will in everything. We are to give up our understanding of the life situations around us and completely lean on God. Rest your whole weight on Him with a surrendered, trusting heart, and He will make you walk in "...the way of life..." (Psalm 16:11). See? His encouragement is as plain as day. He tells it like it is—He is truthful in love.

Last for now (but not least), Romans 8:38-39 (NIV): "And I am convinced that nothing can ever separate us from God's love. Neither death nor life, neither angels nor demons, neither our fears for today nor our worries about tomorrow—not even the powers of hell can separate us from God's love. No power in the sky above or in the earth below—indeed, nothing in all creation will ever be able to separate us from the love of God that is revealed in Christ

Jesus our Lord." Does that blow your mind or what?! *Nothing* (I would triple the italics on that one if I had the option!) can pull God's phenomenal, never-ending, unfailing, faithful love away from us, not even the most daunting and powerful forces. God's love is *that* heavy on us. We can't escape it, not even if we tried. We can run, but we can't hide! Now that's a God who cares! No earthly love would be able to withstand those factors; His love is greater than anything else. Are you encouraged or are you encouraged?! You should be. God loves you, you know that?

Paul mentions in several of his letters that we believers, as the body of Christ, should be encouraging each other in our walks with the Lord (2 Corinthians 13:11, 1 Thessalonians 4:18, 1 Thessalonians 5:11, Hebrews 3:13, Hebrews 10:25), but how exactly can we do that if we don't read the Bible? First off all, is our definition of encouragement in sync with what the Bible shows to be encouragement? For starters, encouragement is not this:

MIKE: Man, I really did horrible on the basketball scrimmage last Tuesday.

KYLE: (thinks, *Yup, thanks to you, we lost.*) What? Oh, uh, no, you were like the best player on the team!

Or this...

ANNE: Do you like my new shirt?

GRACE: (thinks, *That is* the ugliest *shirt I've ever laid eyes on!*) Girl, I'm jealous! That is the cutest shirt I've ever seen! Love it!

Encouragement is not to be mixed up with flattery, and it should not conflict with truthfulness. True encouragement should be words of edification and praise said at the appropriate time that build the other person up in their walk with the Lord. More like:

> **ADDY:** Hey, great talk on honesty. I think the youth group really got a lot out of that; I know I did.
>
> **GREYSON:** Thanks, Addy. I pray that they did. God has really been pointing that subject out to me lately.

Or…

> **DONOVAN:** Lee, I just wanted to let you know that I've noticed the helpful attitude you've been showing Mom today. Keep up the good work.
>
> **LEE:** (probably a little shocked) Uh… thanks, Donny!

We not only *get* encouragement from God's Word, but we learn how to truly encourage others, as well. Encouragement, especially when done spontaneously, should be Spirit-lead (in other words, we should feel prompted by the Holy Spirit in us to speak up, not just give a compliment on our own strength). Occasionally, one way to encourage others is to empathize with them in a struggle or trial. For example:

> **TIMOTHY:** I don't know why, but I've really been struggling with controlling my temper lately.
>
> **ROBERT:** Hey, man, don't be discouraged. That's been a struggle of mine for a while, actually, and I've found some effective verses and methods for coping with it. I'll be praying for you.

Or...

> **MAKIYA:** I've been really down lately because my grandma
> died a few weeks ago. I was really close to her.
> **ANNABELLE:** I'm so sorry, Makiya. I can totally relate with
> what you're going through. My grandpa died about two
> years ago, and I felt the same way.

Encouragement is such a great concept. We serve an amazingly
smart God who came up with the greatest ideas. Speaking of
encouragement, I hope you'll find the information in this next
section as encouraging as I did!

TANGIBLE PROOF

Sometimes I wish I could take everything that God says by faith
without raising questions. Jesus did, after all, say, "...Blessed are those
who believe without seeing me" (John 20:29). Yet, God also knew
the kinds of questions and doubts that would surround us. It amazes
me how much tangible evidence points to God's amazing truth!

I can't pretend to be a Science or History expert, but I'll tell
you one thing: God is. For instance, did you know that the Bible
stated the earth's round shape way before scientists figured it out[3]?
Read for yourself, Isaiah 40:22, "God sits above the circle of the
earth..." Interesting, huh? I strongly encourage you to look up
more apologetics facts, like the reliability of the Bible. You'll be
blown away at how solid our faith is!

3   Lisle, Dr. Jason. "Taking Back Astronomy." *Answers Update.* Answers in Genesis. 1 June 2006. Web. 23 Nov. 2013
    http://www.answersingenesis.org/articles/au/taking-back-astronomy

Does it make you happy or does it make you happy to know that we serve a God who is real?! And He so wanted people to know how real He is that He left us plenty of proof of His existence and His work (study apologetics to find out the nitty-gritty, tangible details of the Christian truths we stand upon, such as the Bible's reliability, Creation, and the existence of God—it is essential to be able to defend your faith). He is so merciful to us!

The Bible is the most mind-bafflingly awe-inspiring, life-changing, light-shedding, heart-penetrating, sin-crushing, love-drenched Book that ever has or ever will exist. Why? Because it's written by God Himself. You see, God used those authors like Moses, Isaiah, Luke, Paul, John, and the others to pen them on the paper, but His Holy Spirit was the Advocate of all the Words that they wrote down (John 14:16, John 15:26, John 16:7). That would be like if I called you over and I dictated all the words of this book to you while you typed. Yes, I still would have written the book without actually placing a finger on the keyboard. Hopefully, that helps clarify how God wrote this infallible Book.

I'll leave you with 2 Timothy 3:14-17 to meditate on: "But you must remain faithful to the things you have been taught. You know they are true, for you know you can trust those who taught you. You have been taught the holy Scriptures from childhood, and they have given you the wisdom to receive the salvation that comes by trusting in Christ Jesus. All Scripture is inspired by God and is useful to teach us what is true and to make us realize what is wrong in our lives. It corrects us when we are wrong and teaches us to do what is right. God uses it to prepare and equip his people to do every good work."

I DARE YOU...

See for yourself. Read what the Book of Psalms says about the Bible. Here's a list of references for you to look up: Psalm 18:30, Psalm 119 (verses 9, 11, 16, 17, 28, 37, 43, 65, 74, 81, 89, 101, 105, 114, 133, 147, 169, 172), and Psalm 130:5. What better way to get your feet wet in Bible reading than by actually reading the Bible where it talks about reading the Bible? God's Word is amazing—I mean, I can't name one other book that changes lives as much, speaks to so many different people in so many different ways, and withstands the test of time. God is a sensational Author.

Look into the apologetics and history of the Bible. I recommend the website *Answers In Genesis* (see the recommendations at the back of the book) for Christian Creationist apologetics. You will find, if you look in the right places, that the Bible is unmatched by any other book. This study will strengthen your faith, build your knowledge, and prepare you to challenge the beliefs of those who doubt or completely dismiss the Bible as inaccurate or as a book written by man alone.

FOOD FOR THOUGHT...

1. Why should we love God's Law and Commandments?

   God did not give us the law so we could be saved through it. God pointed to a Savior who alone could save us. By giving us a law and commandments to live by God helps... (1) To restrain sin. (2) Makes us aware of sin and the need for grace. Romans 7:7 (NIV1984): "What shall we say, then? Is the law sin? Certainly not! Indeed I would not have known what sin was except through the law. For I would not have known what coveting really was if the law had not said, "Do not covet." *And (3) it reveals the Heart of God and the duty of man.* Galatians 3:24 (NIV1984): "So the law was put in charge to lead us to Christ that we might be justified by faith." —BAILEY, AGE 15

2. Why should we, as believers, strive to know God personally?

   (1) You aren't a believer unless you know God personally. (2) The closer you are to God the easier it is going to make life. (3) You cannot make it on your own without God. (4) God wants to be close to you. (5) You want to be closer to God because He created you to be close to Him. (6) He is a wonderful Daddy. —PERRY, AGE 14

3. What are the benefits of being equipped with the Word of God?

One of the benefits of having memorized Scripture is that the Lord can bring verses to your mind when you need them, such as when you are tempted, scared, need encouragement, or defending your faith. —ERIN, AGE 17

4. What are some ways that the Lord speaks to us?

As a Christian, God speaks to us through His Word and the Holy Spirit. —ROBBY, AGE 14

5. What does true, practical encouragement look like?

I would say that true encouragement is building up someone's faith. Words have a lot of power, and just telling someone that they can make it, that they can do it... It can have a momentous outcome on one's faith. Just speaking words of positivity into one's life will do so much for someone. —OLIVIA, AGE 14

CHAPTER 11
The How

Don't Commit Only to Quit

A little over two years ago, I made a commitment to read the Bible every day for the rest of my life. I am pleased to say that I haven't missed more than five days in all that time. In fact, I am glad that I chose to make such a commitment. It is one of the best decisions anyone could ever make. I hope and pray that you, too, decide to commit to reading the Bible everyday. We've talked about several reasons why we should read the Bible, but now it's time to get practical and explore just how this can all be feasibly done.

First of all, you have to be all in. A commitment isn't going to stick so well if you don't strongly believe in your reasons for following through with it. Nearly all of us have observed the common custom of making and then breaking resolutions about, oh, a month after the New Year… and, for the truly half-committed, maybe two months. Maybe Titus committed to go to the gym five mornings a week, but then he decided he liked the donut shop next door much better. Maybe Thelma was pumped with enthusiasm about her new no-sodas-sugar-chips-transfats-or-corn syrup diet, but after discovering her new love of Little Debbie cakes, her excitement dwindled. Or, maybe Clint decided that he wanted to read the Bible everyday—and, pretty soon, he came up with his new slogan—"You lost me at Leviticus."

Let this chapter be a great bank of suggestions and tips. I am throwing out all sorts of ideas onto the table for you to evaluate, pray about, consider, try, and find out what works best for you and your situation. There is no one "right method" or "right order" to Bible reading, as long as you are seeking the Lord with all of your heart, hungering and thirsting for His Word.

Rumor has it that it takes about twenty-one days to form a habit, but I hear that it takes a lot less time to break one. How do we avoid making a commitment on a whim only to break it days later? Accountability, for one, is an effective way to keep up with our promises. Ask your parents, siblings, or a friend to frequently remind you (maybe send you a message once a day, include it as a "chore" on your to-do list for a period of time, or give you a call). You could do the same for them. That way, there is a mutual sense of teamwork on this great venture to read the Bible daily.

Many ministries nowadays offer email subscriptions that will send you a Bible verse or portion of the Bible daily or on weekdays straight to your email inbox. You could set an alarm as a reminder. Lure yourself with a reward saved for the end of a week or month that you were faithful with your commitment without missing a day (like use a candy bar as a bookmark—definitely not the most healthy option, but it would be effective for me).

The truth is, when we make a commitment, we've got to want to keep it. We can't expect our promises to fulfill themselves. You and

I, we can do this. But do we want to? As for me, I've already made the decision to read the Bible every day, whether I want to or not (though the funny thing is, I find myself craving His Word quite often). How about you? What will you choose?

GOOD MORNING

Those are the words that run through my head as my alarm clock begins to sing *Deep In the Heart of Texas* at six in the morning. Those same thoughts lead me to set my alarm clock for another ten minutes. And another. And another... until finally, it's been half an hour since I purposed the night before to get up and read the Bible. As for me, I'm not a morning person. Did that sound sort of like that scenario I described to you at the very beginning of this book? It should. But this one is my story.

Up until recently, my personal Bible time (aside from schoolwork and church) usually looked like reading a couple verses from various books and chapters in the evening. But now I see that perhaps I should have been doing things a tad differently. Now, don't get me wrong, I know that for some people's situations, the evening is the only time all day that they have to slow down and spend time with God. But, not that long ago, I was prompted by the Lord that, perhaps, I should begin spending time with the Him in the morning. Instead of just ending my day with fellowship with God and making it the last thing I do in the day, I should be starting my day in the Word and making it the first thing I do.

Many verses in Scripture mention fellowshipping with the Lord in the morning (italics mine): "The entire family got up *early the next morning* and went to worship the Lord..." (1 Samuel 1:19); "He faced the square just inside the Water Gate from *early morning* until noon and read aloud to everyone who could understand. All the people listened closely to the Book of the Law" (Nehemiah 8:3); "Satisfy us *each morning* with your unfailing love, so we may sing for joy to the end of our lives" (Psalm 90:14); "*Before daybreak the next morning,* Jesus got up and went out to an isolated place to pray" (Mark 1:35); "The crowds gathered at the Temple *early each morning* to hear him [Jesus]" (Luke 21:38; brackets mine); "...but *early the next morning* he [Jesus] was back again at the Temple. A crowd soon gathered, and he sat down and taught them" (John 8:2; brackets mine).

Well, you get the idea. Back to my beginning story: The first morning I tried this new= method, I woke up, prayed for the day ahead of me, decided to begin working through Romans (I read Romans 1 the first day), wrote a little summary on the chapter in my Bible journal, wrote out a key verse from that chapter, and I read from a few devotionals. And the result? I really felt refreshed from that early time in God's Word (you fellow non-morning people know how rare it is for us to actually feel refreshed in the morning!). I ended in prayer, and I went about my day. In the evening, I skimmed over the chapter I had read in the morning, and I jumped around the Bible reading a few verses I had previously highlighted. I also decided that I wanted to begin working on memorizing Scripture.

Bible reading is one of the most vital keys to our Christian walk. Daily Bible reading is essential to the life of a believer. We need to be feeding our spiritual person with spiritual food, or else we will get spiritually sick from starvation. They say that breakfast is supposed to be the biggest meal we eat all day. I guess we could compare having our Bible time in the morning to a Spiritual breakfast! Would you like to join me on this fight against sleepiness, and wake up in the morning to read God's Word? It'd be awfully nice to have some moral support.

A Plethora of Plans

There are a trillion daily Bible reading plans out there. Not sure where to start? Keep in mind when you are searching for a Bible plan (especially if you are new to daily Bible reading) not to over exert yourself with more than you can or will read. You don't want to become so frustrated with your plan that you decide to dump it and skip a day (or several!). The point of daily Bible reading is to keep spiritually fit, continually growing in your relationship with the Lord, and fellowshipping with Him by eating your spiritual meals— *not* to have a spiritual Thanksgiving pig-out feast where you cram so much food down your throat without even chewing that it loses flavor and you feel sick afterwards. Not the point at all. In other words, consider your daily circumstances (like, maybe you have a bus to catch at 7:45 or you work early hours) and find a *doable plan*.

For a daily plan, I have taken to reading one chapter of the Bible every morning. As I mentioned before, I started in Romans, and I am just working my way upward. You could start at Genesis and read one chapter of the Bible a day. It may take a while to work through all sixty-six books, but you will have plenty of time to process the information you read, given such a short portion. Some places to look for more systematic reading plans would be Bible Gateway and YouVersion. I strongly suggest audio Bibles, as well.

Now, aside from daily reading, I'm going to share with you a favorite plan of mine that I have tested myself (and have highly benefited from!). It's a plan my mom came up with for my home-schooling. Here's what you do: Three days a week, you read nine pages from the Bible each of those days, starting in Genesis, and working straight through to Revelation. On Bible Gateway and YouVersion (see the recommendations at the back of the book), you can listen to the audio as you read along (you can also buy audio discs by *Zondervan* and such). What works best for me is to listen along with headphones to the audio as I hold an actual paper-paged Bible (not an eReader) with a pen and/or highlighter in hand to underline verses that stand out to me. Personally, I don't like taking notes as I listen (occasionally, when I have an epiphany right in the moment, I scrawl a little note down in the margins of my Bible), but maybe that works for you. I have a composition notebook where I write the date and the chapters I listened to and read. You will finish the Bible in less than a year!

At first, especially after Genesis and the beginning of Exodus (those are very good, audience-gripping books, actually), you may get a little antsy just sitting there (I did), especially through some of the less fast-paced books. When I began getting very impatient,

I would doodle in the journal that I tracked my reading in. While it helped sometimes, I lost my concentration other times. There were occasionally times when I had to reread a chapter or two. That's just the way I'm wired; it could be a different scenario for you. Also, listening to the Bible on audio while cooking, cleaning, working, and the like are great ideas, but for this plan's reading, I found it very hard to concentrate while multitasking. I think I let First and Second Chronicles fly right past me as I curled my hair!

After a while, you may begin to realize how close you are growing to the Lord and what a love you are cultivating for His Word! In fact, beginning this plan is what inspired me to write this book! God's Word is so alive and so colorful, you may find yourself honestly confessing that, yes, the Bible is your new favorite book!

Conversion to a New Version

The Bible is the true Word of God, no doubt about it. However, as it has been translated from Hebrew and Greek into a bounty of different languages by different people from different denominations with different opinions, interpretations, and points of view, it is necessary to be mindful of which Bible version(s) we choose to read from. Ultimately, I can't tell you which version to read or to not read, because, number one, that choice is strictly up to your family. Some families stick straight to one version, others will prefer certain ones over the rest, while even others like to read from a broad variety of versions.

When looking for the "perfect version," it may be helpful to find articles by the translators giving more information about what changes they have recently added and why, what makes their version unique, and so on. I did that when we were having questions about recent revisions made to a certain version we had been using. If you have trouble finding a reliable version, talk to a godly, Christian adult (your parents, pastor, youth pastor, etc.) for version suggestions. Selecting the best version of Scripture to read may be a scholarly question best answered by your trusted pastor or mentor. A good safeguard to set in place would be to read out of multiple versions (as I mentioned before), and compare the translations. In fact, you might even get more out of the verses you read if you read them from different angles and interpretations.

Two of the versions I like to use include the Amplified Bible (AMP) and the New Living Translation (NLT). The AMP's verses provide the Greek and Hebrew definitions to a word, making the Scripture and its meaning a lot clearer and easier to understand. I enjoy reading the Amplified Bible when I want to "wring out" a verse/chapter to its full worth. The NLT also tries to convey the Greek and Hebrew meanings in a clear, simple way. Among others, these are a few of my favorites.

Journalism 101

Journals, contrary to popular belief, are not just for girls. They're simply blank books with space to write in—very convenient for Bible reading and prayer time. See, sometimes when we are reading, we may have a profound insight into God's Word whack us in the head, and we won't want to forget it. And what if we hear that still, small voice whispering an inspiration? Or, what if we find a meaty chapter full of key verses and applicable points for our life and situation?

What to do, what to do… I know! Let's explore the vast possibilities set before us when we pick up a practice called journaling.

I keep a both Bible journal and a prayer/idea journal that I write in every once in a while; it's not something I do every single time I have morning or evening devotions. This, personally, for me differs from regular journaling. In a regular journal, I would right down the activities I did that day, the food I ate, the places I went, and the people I met. It would be kind of like a history essay of my day. For me, I like to do things differently with my Bible and prayer/idea journals:

In my Bible journal, I might write down something I sensed that the Lord spoke to me, a key verse(s), and/or a summary of the chapter I read. In fact, I would especially recommend that you try (at least once!) writing a summary of the chapter you read. Sometimes there are so many different ideas, concepts, topics, facets, and angles being presented in one chapter alone, that it leaves me kind of scatterbrained and not quite able to pinpoint the main subject I just read about. Writing an essay ties the strings and draws connections between the verses.

In my prayer/idea journal, I will usually write down prayer

requests or a rough outline of what I am going to pray about. Sometimes I will even write out prayers to the Lord like a letter. The reason I wrote "prayer/*idea*" journal is because I will write down ideas that I perceive the Lord to be giving me. Here's a highly relevant example: I would write down ideas in my prayer/idea journal for topics for a certain book I was planning on writing. Guess which topic I decided on?

Journaling is not something that I have committed to doing regularly. Though I am a big writer, I am not a very big journalist. Sometimes, for me, if I plan beforehand on journaling every time I have my morning devotions, I begin to dread the Bible reading time or just want it to be "over with"—to check it off of my checklist. Ecclesiastes 8:3 (NIV) has been a help in keeping my time of devotions in perspective: "Do not be in a hurry to leave the king's presence…"

Study Buddies

Let me share with you some of my most favorite tools for Bible studying: journals, pens, highlighters, devotionals, and multiple versions of Bibles. I use every single one of these when I'm trying to milk my Bible reading time for all its worth. I especially endorse the highlighter (or pen)—believe it or not, I feel like I'm catching fish without a net when I read the Word without something to underline and write with. You see, sometimes I'll be reading along, soaking in the words, when all of a sudden I see a verse that I never, ever want to forget, so I grab a pen and underline the verse, and—if it's really good—I'll circle the number and/or draw an arrow pointing to it. Anything to draw my attention to it the next time I am passing through that page.

During church, I like to take notes on the sermon. Not only does it help me to remember what was said later on, but I tend to get more out of the message, as well. At the very least, I'm getting good practice for college. On the subject of church, plugging into a good body of believers (church) is beneficial for our spiritual walk. I once met a girl that said, "Yeah, I believe in Jesus, but I don't think you have to go to church to be a Christian." I responded, "Going to church definitely does not make you a Christian, but it is good to be a part of a body of believers to encourage you in your walk with the Lord." Plugging into a church is one of the opportunities God has placed before us to learn more about Him, grow in His Word, surround ourselves with Christians and godly counsel, and become fruitful in our spiritual lives. No church is the perfect church, but the Lord has somewhere for you where He plans to water the seeds in your heart. In addition to church, places like youth groups, conferences, small groups, and Bible studies are other ways to be working the soil in our hearts.

Another great study option is to read out of multiple Bible versions (say, two or three) and compare the same verse. I especially like to do that when I don't understand a verse in one translation. I simply switch to another and (hopefully) find a little more clarity or explanation! Devotionals, especially the day-by-day ones, give words of encouragement and nuggets of Scripture to gnaw on throughout the day.

Have you ever asked your Christian friends what the Lord has been doing in their lives or speaking to/teaching them? Have you ever asked them if there is anything you can be praying for them about? Have you discussed Scripture, spiritual things, and the Lord with them? I've got to admit, this is a very new concept for me. But, as I've been recently discovering, it draws friends together in such a deeper way (it also can help you to see which friends are ones worth having). When you are seeking God with others who care about Him as much as you do, it's no longer just you seeking and studying God's Word—it's a group of believers in search of spiritual treasure. You challenge one another to dig deeper. You learn from one another. You shape one another for good. Seeking the Lord and studying His Holy Book alone is great... difficult, but great. But doing that together? Even better.

Reading the Bible everyday of our life for the rest of our life sounds like an intimidating task at first. But, really, there are 1,440 minutes each day that most people waste away on social media, TV, video games, and the like. Surely, the God of the Universe deserves much more than our minimal "once in a while" fickle Bible reading and our one hour forty-five minutes at church on Sunday mornings. The Bible has so much potential to change our life (even if you are a believer already). I strongly encourage you to make a commitment to the Lord to read the Bible everyday—spending time in His Word and fellow-shipping with Him. Such a small sacrifice for such a worthy King! His Word is alive (Hebrews 4:12)! Don't give up if consistency is hard at first. It's hard for all of us. Know that you are not alone. Remember James 1:22-24, a good reminder for all of us on what Bible reading is truly about (italics mine): "But don't just listen to God's word. You must *do what it says*. Otherwise, you are only fooling yourselves. For if you listen to the word and don't obey, it is like glancing at your face in a mirror. You see yourself, walk away, and forget what you look like."

I DARE YOU...

If you haven't already, I highly recommend that you purpose to read the Bible every day. But, I must warn you, commitments aren't something to take lightly. Read the Old Testament, and you'll find out that God doesn't like empty vows (Deuteronomy 23:21,23). God already knows every element of your being, but He wants you to know Him! He really, really loves you, and He wants to talk with you! His love is so mind-boggling, because we don't deserve it and we have trouble imagining just how humongous it is (Ephesians 3:17-19)! Ponder just how amazing His love is. Hands down, He deserves our all.

I had never really talked that much about spiritual matters with my Christian friends—usually, most of my conversations weren't very "deep." But, as I mentioned before, that has changed recently, because the Lord has been bringing friends into my life that have challenged me to be doing more of that. Ask your friends how their spiritual walk is going, how you can pray for them, what the Lord has been teaching them, or something similar. I must admit, when I started getting asked questions like that, I was thrown a bit off guard.

I didn't have that much to say because I really hadn't thought about it. Even if they don't give you a very eloquent, "heartfelt" answer, you can rest assured that there's an eighty percent chance they were challenged to have an answer ready for the next time you asked. For sake of being included, they'll probably seek the Lord more seriously and discover something even greater than a new conversation topic.

FOOD FOR THOUGHT...

1. What is the most rewarding thing about reading the Bible?

    You get to know Jesus better. —ADEN, AGE 9

2. What are the advantages of reading the Bible in the morning?

    I would say one of the biggest advantages of reading your Bible in the morning is that it sets you in the right mindset for the rest of the day. When you start your day with God in mind, it makes it a more prevalent thought in your head as you deal with the situations throughout the day. —KURT, AGE 16

3. What is your favorite way to study God's Word?

    My favorite way to study the Bible is when I am alone and read my Bible. When we do a lesson at church it is good, but when I am alone God says something to just me personally. I like to read the Bible in my bedroom, with my dog, then think my own thoughts about what God is saying, and God listens to me. —JOY, AGE 13

4. Why should we find a body of fellow believers to be a part of?

I think it's important to have a group of people with the same goals. It's really hard to live like Jesus wants us to without seeing it done in other people. It's good to have the encouragement to keep pressing forward. —TESSA, AGE 16

5. In what ways can we encourage and challenge others in their walk with Christ?

Just by expressing God in everything we do. When we're right with Him, we have a special Presence in our spirit. And God is flowing out of us. So basically just walking with God all the days of our lives. Recently I have had to make Jesus mine… and not just my parents. I read and found out why I believe what I do. And why we do things. And that has changed my life. —KATE, AGE 14

CHAPTER 12
Do You Know the Author?

THE FATE OF THE FAITHLESS

MATTHEW 7:21-23

This place is breathtaking! Absolutely grand! And there He is! There, up on His throne! A young man walked up an echoing corridor towards a magnificent room with a King on His throne. *Click, click.* The sound of his steady walk rung up and down the halls. As the man got closer and closer to the throne itself, he strained his eyes to see the King's face. He blinked. He strained some more. Something in the King's face made the man a little nervous. His heart began beating a notch faster.

Finally, the man was standing before the very King Himself. Something in the King's vibrant eyes looked grave. Something in His shining face looked glum. Something in His powerful voice frightened the man.

"Why should I accept you into My Kingdom?" the King's voice boomed.

The young man straightened himself up to his full six-foot-one height, looked the King in the eye, and said, "*Lord! Lord! I prophesied in your name and cast out demons in your name and performed many miracles in your name*" (Matthew 7:22).

The King sighed and shook His head. "You're not the first one to give me *that* answer." The young man's heart began pounding in his ears. The King's response couldn't have been good. The man began to quiver violently and tears began to pour from his eyes uncontrollably. A tangling mess of knots formed in his throat and in the deep pit of his stomach. He was terrified.

"*I never knew you. Get away from me, you who breaks God's laws*" (Matthew 7:23). The King, saying this, then turned His grief-stricken face away from the pale young man—one of many, many people who would be tasting true death and eternal separation from the Light.

The man hyperventilated, and his knees became as weak as threads—he thought they might give way. He shook with agony and fear. He began to sweat terribly. Falling to his knees, the poor soul cried, "No! No, please! No!" As two guards dragged him off to his forever death—an execution sentence so permanent and dreadful that it sends chills up and down the spine just trying to fathom it—he knew that the only thing worse than his eternal sentence to hell, the dark place with *weeping and gnashing of teeth* (Matthew 8:12), would be his eternal separation from the King of kings, whom He had not followed while there was still time.

Ten Lies About Salvation

Sadly, the young man in the story isn't the only one who has or will meet this tragic fate. Not everyone will enter into the Kingdom of Heaven. There will be people that will, in fact, go to the very real, very horrendous place called hell. The Author of the Bible, of the Universe, and of your life—the Father who loves you, the Friend who longs to fellowship with you—He is also a just judge who will fairly sift the righteous followers from the sinful from His throne. Tell me, where are you going after you die? Are you sure about your destination?

Satan's goal is to destroy your soul. He wants you to go to hell, because those who go to hell will be eternally separated from God, just as he will. He's made up plenty of convincing lies and traps to keep people from Jesus's salvation. Here are ten of the biggest lies around:

1. *I'm a Christian because my mom/dad is a Christian.*

   Wrong. God doesn't have grandchildren. Salvation is individual—each of us has to make our own choice to follow Christ.

2. *I'm a Christian because I feel that God is here with me.*

   God is everywhere. Salvation isn't just a feeling—sometimes, it's not even a feeling at all. To say that you are a Christian simply because you have a feeling that God is with you won't make the cut.

3. *I am a good person. I deserve to go to Heaven.*

But are you really? Look at the Ten Commandments (read Exodus 20:1-21). Have you broken any of those rules? So have I. So, according to the Law, we are liars, thieves, idolaters, and the like. Should God let us Law-breakers into Heaven with the criminal record we have? No. But He is a merciful God, and because of His great decision to send Jesus as our ransom, we have hope. Read on to find out about this hope. So, mankind isn't basically good, then? Romans 3:23 assures us that it isn't: "For everyone has sinned; we all fall short of God's glorious standard." We're all sinners, all in need of a Savior. Nobody "deserves" to go to Heaven. Humans are born with a sinful nature, thanks to Adam and Eve's decision to go against God's commands way back at the beginning of time in the Garden of Eden (Genesis 3).

4. *God is too good to send anyone to hell.*

We both agree that God is good. Well, part of His goodness is His justice—He is fair. So, He is also a just judge. And, as a just judge, He will administer justice to whom it is due. Isaiah 30:18 (NIV) says, "...For the Lord is a God of justice..." Those who are deserving of hell (which includes all of us) will be thrown into hell (a very real, very devastating place)—unless, of course, they repent and turn to follow Jesus. But we haven't gotten to that part yet.

5. *I've done a lot more good stuff in my life than bad. God will let it slide.*

If you've seen the Christian movie *Courageous*[4] (Sherwood Pictures), you may remember the scene where Officer Nathan Hayes witnesses to a distressed fellow policeman, David Thomson. When David hears that everyone will have to stand before God on Judgment day, he responds by saying that he hopes that his good outweighs his bad. Nathan uses an analogy that goes something like this: Who is person that you feel that you are closest to? (David answered that he was closest to his mom.) What if that person was attacked and murdered in a parking lot, and the bad guy was caught and put on trial— and the bad guy tells the judge, "Look, judge, I committed this crime, but I've done a lot of good in my life." If that judge lets the man free, would you say he was a good judge or a bad judge? (David said a bad one.) This analogy holds true. God is a good judge, and, as you know from the answer to number five, he is a just judge and he will not let the guilty go without punishment. The "good" done in one's life will not lighten the punishment or affect in any way what they did wrong.

6. *I think that there are many ways to get to Heaven. Lots of religions (if not all) will give you eternal life.*

Other religions will give you eternity...in hell. It takes a little bit of studying world religions to realize that many of those

---

4   *Courageous.* Prod. Stephen Kendrick. Dir. Alex Kendrick. Tristar Pictures & Sherwood Pictures, 2011.

religions are, in fact, quite conflicting with one another. Some of those people will say, "Oh, Jesus was a good teacher." Would a good teacher *lie?* So, when Jesus said, "I am the way, the truth, and the life. No one can come to the Father except through me," in John 14:6, was He lying? No. There is no way to eternal life but by Jesus, and Jesus alone. Anything contrary to that would be breaking the first commandment and defying Jesus's words in Matthew 6:24: "No one can serve two masters. For you will hate one and love the other; you will be devoted to one and despise the other..." Another difference is that, in Christianity, the God of the universe has reached out to mankind and has made a way for salvation only by His grace through faith in Jesus. All other religions require man to look for God and achieve salvation through a set of rules.

7. *There is no god. We just live and have fun while it lasts, then we die. Period.*

Yes, there is a God. There are many people that will die without ever believing this, but after that, they will know that there was, and is, in fact, a God who loved them and wanted to save them, but it will be too late for them because they will already be dead. I know that sometimes Christians, in our faith, waver, and we begin to wonder, *So, is He really, truly real?* There is scientific, historical, tangible evidence that points to His existence. God knew that it would be hard for us to believe in One we can't experience with our five physical senses. When we, as Christians, struggle in our faith (like, we know He's real in our hearts, but we are constantly warring against thoughts that are telling us that He's not), we need to share the same response as the father of the demon-possessed boy who doubted: "I do believe, but help me overcome my unbelief!" (Mark 9:24; The whole story can be found in Mark 9:14-29) I find that verse to be so encouraging—here we are, humans with a nature that wants to revolt against God, yet we choose to believe and cry out to the Lord to help us conquer that doubt. But, doubt in believers is a different discussion. If you are a non-believer and you share this view of God, I encourage you to read up on the apologetics in favor of God and His Son's existence. It may blow your mind.

8. *Yeah, I'm a Christian! I go to church on Sundays (or on Easter and Christmas) and I honk every time I see a "Honk if you love Jesus!" bumper sticker. I even have some Christmas pencils with the manger, the wise men, and the bright star!*

As funny and wild as we can get with the examples of "Christianity" (i.e., I have a WWJD bracelet from my first grade year at VBS and a cross necklace I won at AWANA, I sang a song written by a Christian guy in church choir, I have Billy Graham's autograph… well, you get the idea), this is sadly a very widespread, popular belief among even the seemingly "Christian," church-going people of the world. Choosing Jesus as our Lord and Savior isn't about what we "do" that looks good spiritual-wise or that makes us look "holy," like telling our English class that our favorite book is the Bible (which it may be, and there's no problem with sharing that, but claiming that simply so we will "look" like Christians and make ourselves feel likes "Christians" is missing the point of the gospel). And, Christianity isn't just about what we "don't" do that gives us "holiness" points, like not drinking, smoking, or doing drugs. Sure, there are things that we as Christians should not do, but we abstain from those things out of our love for Christ, our joy that He has saved us, and our desire to serve, please, and honor His holy Name!

9. *I can earn my way to Heaven by good works!*

Then how, exactly, did the criminal hanging on the cross next to Jesus get into Heaven? He was hours, if not minutes, if not *seconds* away from his final breath. He had lived a life full of crime and sinfulness, and now, the Romans were putting him to death. He didn't have another chance to earn a ticket to

Heaven by good works. He couldn't have climbed off the cross to feed the poor or to love his neighbor. Yet, on his last day, Jesus admitted the man into Heaven. "Then he [the criminal] said, "Jesus, remember me when you come into your Kingdom." And Jesus replied, "I assure you, today you will be with me in paradise" (Luke 23:42-43; brackets mine). You don't have to take my word for it—read the story for yourself in Luke 23:32-43.

10. *How do I think I can achieve eternal life? Well, I need Jesus and my good works.*

Buzzz. That was the wrong answer (and it was not the same answer as number nine, in case you were wondering). That one might have thrown you off a little! It did to me, too, when I read something similar. The thing is, Jesus is the only One that can save us and grant us eternal life. If we rely on Jesus *plus* our good works, then we are saying that Jesus Christ, the Son of God who died so that we might live, is not enough to save us. This incorrect belief states that we need good works, too, in order to obtain salvation.

The truth is, not one of us can earn our salvation. It is a completely free gift from God. I like how the Amplified Bible (AMP) expands on Ephesians 2:8-10 (brackets, parentheses, and italics from AMP): "For it is by free grace (God's unmerited favor) that you are saved (delivered from judgment *and* made partakers of Christ's salvation) through [your] faith. And this [salvation] is not of yourselves [of your own doing, it came not through your own striving], but it is the gift of God; Not because of works [not the fulfillment of the Law's demands], lest any man should boast. [It is not the result of what anyone can possibly do, so no one can pride himself in it or take glory to himself.] For we are God's [own] handiwork (His workmanship), recreated in Christ Jesus, [born anew] that we may do those good works which God predestined (planned beforehand) for us [taking paths which He prepared ahead of time], that we should walk in them [living the good life which He prearranged and made ready for us to live]."

Are You Perfect Enough?

Ladies and gentlemen, young and old! Come one, come all, to *Heaven!* Only two types of people can get into this glorious place of eternal life. The first kind of person is a *perfect person*. In other words, you must have kept all Ten Commandments all of your life! But, there is a minor (or should I say, major) glitch in this requirement: *no human is perfect!* Again, Romans 3:23: "For everyone has sinned; we all fall short of God's glorious standard."

Yep, let's face it: you and I have broken several of the Ten Commandments. It's the truth. We've all told a lie before (possibly multiple times every day), we've all hated someone before (Jesus counts hatred as murder, remember?), and we've all stolen before (maybe physically, like keeping the extra twenty bucks that the cashier accidentally handed us, or maybe spiritually, like stealing someone's dream or joy by quenching it). So there we have it—we may be upstanding citizens on the outside, or in the world's eyes, but we're pretty dirty criminals according to God's standards! Would *you* let a liar, murderer, and thief into Heaven if you were the judge? Well, who would?

But guess what—(I'm about to tell you some really great news, so pay extra close attention!) we have hope. The second kind of person allowed into Heaven is a person with Jesus living in his or her heart. Think about this with me for a second—Jesus is the only perfect person—the Son of God! If God looks at our hearts and sees *not* a criminal record of breaking the Law, but His Own blameless Son living within us, He will allow us into His marvelous Kingdom. You see, sin was separating us from God, and we were unable to reach Him. But, God chose to be a merciful Judge to His rebelling people by making a bridge over that chasm of sin so that we can live with Him forever—but we'll get to that in a minute.

Born Again

One night, Jesus revealed the key to being saved in his talk with Pharisee Nicodemus. He said, "I tell you the truth, unless you are born again, you cannot see the Kingdom of God" (John 3:3). Well, that certainly caught Nicodemus by surprise! Like the rest of us would, he had a couple questions to ask on that matter. John 3:4 says, "What do you mean?" exclaimed Nicodemus. "How can an old man go back into his mother's womb and be born again?" Jesus explained to him that to go to Heaven, one must be born twice: first of flesh (so far, so good), then of Spirit. Our sinful human flesh nature must be reborn into the Spirit, which is the Lord (John 3:5-6). We must be born into God's family. Period. (You can read all of John 3 for the full story of Nicodemus and Jesus's conversation)

Let's make sure we're all on the same page here. According to the Bible, we are all sinners condemned to death with an eternal fate in hell, *unless* we accept our Savior, Jesus. I can't wait any longer—let me tell you what Jesus did for us.

A Price So High

The popular Bible verse, John 3:16, ties this story up so well: "For God loved the world so much that he gave his one and only Son, so that everyone who believes in him will not perish but have eternal life." God sent Jesus to die a horrendous death in our place so that we wouldn't have to. You see, the only way for our ransom to be paid and for us to be set free from the chains of sin and death is for a perfect person to die for our sins as a sacrifice. Before Jesus came to earth, the Israelites had to sacrifice a perfect lamb (without any blemishes or deformities) on an altar for their sins. But then, God sent His Lamb, Jesus, to be slaughtered on a cross for our sins. Is this making sense? God loved us so much (far more than we ever deserved!) that He allowed His Own Son to be mocked, spat upon, flogged (beaten hard with a whip), nailed naked to a wooden cross with a crown of thorns stuck upon His head, laughed at by a crowd of people as He hung there between two criminals with a sign over His head reading, "Jesus of Nazareth, the King of the Jews," (John 19:19), and die (Mark 10:34). God charged Jesus with the sins of the *world* as He was dying on the cross (can you imagine how heavy that would be?). Jesus also took all sicknesses and all diseases upon Him (Matthew 8:17).

Can you imagine what Jesus was going through? The Bible says that before He was arrested, Jesus prayed, "Father, if You are willing, please take this cup of suffering away from Me. Yet I want Your will to be done, not Mine" (Luke 22:42). In fact, He was so distressed in His prayer time that He began to sweat drops of blood (which as a very rare actual medical condition when someone is deeply worrying)(Luke 22:44). Then, Matthew 27:46 shows how distressed Jesus was on the cross as He bore our sins: "At about three o'clock, Jesus called out with a loud voice, *"Eli, Eli, lema sabach-thani?"* which means "My God, my God, why have you abandoned me?" He went through all that for *you and I.* Does that make you feel so amazingly special?! It should.

John 19:30: "When Jesus had tasted it, he said, "It is finished!" Then he bowed his head and released his spirit." There. The grave was satisfied. Jesus paid our ransom. We were set free. But wait until you hear what happened next: "At that moment the curtain in the sanctuary of the Temple was torn in two, from top to bottom. The earth shook, rocks split apart, and tombs opened. The bodies of many godly men and women who had died were raised from the dead. They left the cemetery after Jesus' resurrection, went into the holy city of Jerusalem, and appeared to many people. The Roman officer and the other soldiers at the crucifixion were terrified by the earthquake and all that had happened. They said, "This man truly was the Son of God!" (Matthew 27:51-54).

EASTER

Do you know why we celebrate Easter? A lot of people don't. It's not about potlucks, egg hunts, candy, painted eggs, Easter bunnies, or little chicks. It's not even about getting non-Christian people to spend one of two Sunday mornings in the year in a church building, or about wearing fancy Sunday clothes. Easter Sunday is a celebration of the best part of the story of salvation.

Jesus didn't stay dead forever. For three days, Jesus's body lay guarded in the tomb of the generous Joseph of Arimathea. The Pharisees wanted to make sure that the disciples didn't try to steal His body to claim that He was risen. So they sealed the tomb and guarded it. They had a pretty fool-proof plan to avoid any phony business or hoaxes. But just wait until you hear what Matthew 28:2-4 says: "Suddenly there was a great earthquake! For an angel of the Lord came down from heaven, rolled aside the stone, and sat on it. His face shone like lightning, and his clothing was as white as snow. The guards shook with fear when they saw him, and they fell into a dead faint." Whoa! So the guards were out cold. But what was going on?

Mary Magdalene and another Mary who had followed Jesus had come to see His tomb, but imagine their surprise to find a shining angel sitting on the stone that was supposed to be guarding their Master's resting place! The angel explained to the women that Jesus was not there anymore; He was *risen*, just like He said He would! The angel showed them where His body had been. As they raced to tell the disciples, they bumped into none other than *Jesus Christ, the Man who had been crucified and resurrected Himself!* If you've ever heard the worship song, *Mighty to Save*[5], one of the lines in the chorus says, *He rose and conquered the grave.* Jesus Christ conquered the grave for you and for me! Can't you see how much God loves us?!

THE MOMENT OF TRUTH

You've probably heard the word, "gospel," before, but did you know that it means, "good news?" When people say, "the Gospel," they

---

5   Hillsong UNITED. "Mighy to Save (Live)." 2010. By Hillsong Church T/A Hillsong Music Australia.*The I Heart Revolution (Live)*. EMI Christian Music Group. 2010, CD.

are referring to the good news that Christ has conquered death and that we, too, can be saved from death and live forever with Jesus, thanks to His death on the cross. Throughout this chapter, I have tried to cover many aspects of salvation and to explain them thoroughly. The Gospel, the way to become a Christian, the way to have eternal life in Heaven—call it what you will, it is a simple, powerful message. Here is the Salvation message in a nutshell:

You and I are sinners. We deserve to die for our sins and be eternally separated from God in hell. Yet, He loved us far too much to let us die, so He made a way for us to be with Him forever by sending His only Son, Jesus Christ, perfect and sinless, to die on the cross for us. He rose from the grave and conquered eternal death. Now, we have the choice to live eternally with Jesus after we die if we "…confess with [our] mouth that Jesus is Lord and believe in [our] heart that God raised him from the dead," for as Romans 10:9 (brackets mine) continues to say, "[we] will be saved." That's the salvation message right there—one short paragraph containing such life transforming news.

Note how the verse said that, "If you *confess with your mouth* that Jesus is Lord and believe in your heart that God raised him from the dead, you will be saved" (Romans 10:9; italics mine) What does it mean to *confess with [our] mouth* (brackets mine)? This means that we need to pray a prayer of salvation. In this prayer, we repent (ask for forgiveness and turn) from our sins to the Lord, declare our need for a Savior, invite Jesus into our heart, and commit our life to following Him. Sound complicated? It's really not. Do you want to pray this prayer to join God's family (Galatians 3:26)? That is the *best* decision you could ever make in your life. By the way, you don't have to worry about using fancy words, correct grammar, or thees and thous. You can talk to God like He's your friend. Not sure how to start? Here's an example prayer for a guide:

> *Dear God, I know I am a sinner. I've done, thought, and said some awful things in my life like ___ , ___ , and ___. Please forgive me of my sins (the bad things I've done, thought, and said) and wash me clean with Jesus's blood. I'm a sinner in need of a Savior, and I can't earn my way into heaven, so I invite Jesus into my heart to be the King and Ruler of my life. From this moment on, I commit to being a follower of Christ. I love you, Father. Thank you for sending Jesus to die for me and for forgiving me. In Jesus's Name, Amen.*

Guess what? If you just invited Jesus into your heart, the angels in heaven are throwing a huge party! Jesus is living on the throne of your heart and you are a Christian! You are a part of God's family! You are my brother- or sister-in-Christ! You have an eternal future in Heaven with the Lord in His Kingdom and in His Holy City, where, "He will wipe every tear from [your] eyes, and there will be no more death or sorrow or crying or pain. All these things are gone forever" (Revelation 21:4; brackets mine).

Stage Two

You, my friend, as an official ambassador for Christ (1 Corinthians 5:20), have a high calling. This means that you and I, as believers, have the tremendous honor of being Jesus's Own representatives! We are privileged to have a difficult and thrilling mission for the Kingdom before us. This calling is called "The Great Commission" (in other words, the great mission), found in Matthew 28:18-20. Read it for yourself: "Jesus came and told his disciples, "I have been given all authority in heaven and on earth. Therefore, go and make disciples of all the nations, baptizing them in the name of the Father and the Son and the Holy Spirit. Teach these new disciples to obey all the commands I have given you. And be sure of this: I am with you always, even to the end of the age."

This little subtitled section is far too small to cover evangelism (y'know, witnessing, sharing the , being fishers of men...) in great depth, but I highly recommend you read other books on the subject (see the recommendations at the back of the book).

In order to grow our spiritual walk, whether we are a "baby Christian" or a veteran in Christianity, we should read the Bible daily, "Never stop praying," (1 Thessalonians 5:17), and turn away from the sinful habits we used to indulge in. If you don't already go to church, find a solid, Gospel believing, Bible rooted church near you. Surround yourself with godly influences, both peers and mentors. Let this be clear: God never said the narrow path (the way of life that we chose to live once we become followers of

God) would be the easy or popular path. In fact, He's said quite the opposite. But you know what else He's said? He said, "God blesses you when people mock you and persecute you and lie about you and say all sorts of evil things against you because you are my followers. Be happy about it! Be very glad! For *a great reward awaits you in heaven...*" (Matthew 5:11-12; italics mine).

If you ever begin losing hope or struggle in your walk and faith and you feel like giving up—when you are asking yourself, "Why did I chose this path? Why am I going through such a painful/hard/trying time? What's the point of following Jesus if I am just going to suffer and be mocked?", remember God's love for you. Remember what He did on the cross for you. Remember the suffering Jesus took for you. Remember the prize ahead of you. Remember that He gave you the Holy Spirit as a Helper. Remember that "The temptations in your life are no different from what others experience. And God is faithful. He will not allow the temptation to be more than you can stand. When you are tempted, he will show you a way out so that you can endure" (1 Corinthians 10:13). Want to know a key to growing close to God? James 4:8 says, "Come close to God, and God will come close to you..."

THE GREATEST BOOK YOU'VE NEVER READ

"Hey, Daddy," I began as I approached my dad with a composition notebook in one hand and a pen in the other. "What should I name my book?"

Casually, he threw out the first clever suggestion that popped in his mind: "*The Greatest Book You've Never Read.*"

Gasp! I scribbled down his idea. "That is perfect!" After His brilliant contribution, I really could not come up with anything better (I hardly tried to—I loved it too much!), so the name stuck. But, you know, this book that you are holding in your hands is not, in fact, the greatest book you've ever (or never) read. This probably wouldn't even rank as one of the top ten greatest books ever (okay, so maybe it ranks eleventh. Just kidding)! But the purpose of this book is to point you to read the *true* greatest book you've never read—the Holy Bible. The Scriptures. God's Word. Our Manual for life. Our Field Guide to life. God's Love Letter to us.

I pray that throughout this book, you have been inspired to read the Bible and that He has kindled a love for His Word in your heart, so that you not only decide to make a personal commitment to reading it daily, but so that you love every minute of it and can't seem to get enough of His Presence! I try my best to describe His awesomeness with adjectives and analogies and all, but I, just as the rest of you, don't even know the beauty of the Holy Bible to its full extent enough to do it justice. I'm merely another child of God learning right alongside my fellow brothers- and sisters-in-Christ.

The Bible, being the divine Word of God, is one of the enemy's favorite targets to spread lies about. He doesn't want you to know it, because he knows that you'll grow in spiritual maturity and in your fervor for the Lord and His Word. Please, don't let Satan win. Don't buy into his lies. He'll throw tricky questions at you like, "So, you actually think the Bible is *reliable?* You actually think an old book like that hasn't been changed so many times that it's not truly God's original Word anymore? You actually believe that this Book is God's Word? You seriously think this book is for us non-pastors?" Plug your ears. Fight back. Need some encouragement?

A faith-booster? We all do. Remember, there is even tangible proof that the Bible is an extremely accurate historical document.

Forgive me, I've kept you too long. We've got a high calling to get to! We have work to do for the Kingdom of Heaven! We have character to build. We have wisdom and knowledge to gain. We have God, family, friends, and even enemies to love. We have people to witness to. We have a faith to defend. But we're not alone. Jesus said He is with us always (remember Matthew 28:20?), and that's the truth. God has sent you the Holy Spirit as a Helper and Teacher (John 14:26). He's given you the glorious honor of being His Own servant. He's given you the Greatest Book You've Never Read.

I DARE YOU...

If you're already a follower of Christ but you haven't been water baptized yet (Matthew 3), look into doing this symbolic act of following the Lord. Baptism certainly does not make you a Christian, just as wearing a medal does not make you a winner. It does, however, symbolize before fellow believers and before God, that you have made the decision to walk the narrow path with Jesus. Romans 6:4 describes this act of obedience well: "For we died and were buried with Christ by baptism. And just as Christ was raised from the dead by the glorious power of the Father, now we also may live new lives." Baptism is not a pool party in a church building, so make sure you understand the meaning of the procedure before doing it.

If you have already committed your life to the Lord, do the chapter 7 dare (the second half). Evangelism is so important. Jesus said, "The harvest is great, but the workers are few" (Matthew 9:37). The Word also says in Romans 10:14-15, "But how can they call on him to save them unless they believe in him? And how can they believe in him if they have never heard about him? And how can they hear about him unless someone tells them? And how will anyone go and tell them without being sent? That is why the Scriptures say, 'How beautiful are the feet of the messengers who bring good news!'" Forget my commentary. Let the Word speak for Itself. As Jesus said in Matthew 4:19, "Come, follow me, and I will show you how to fish for people!" *Go fish!*

FOOD FOR THOUGHT...

1. Why do you think it is important that we realize and acknowledge that we are sinners?

   We need to know that we are sinners so that Jesus can come into our hearts. We have to admit and believe and confess.
   —MOLLY, AGE 11

2. What makes Christianity different from other religions?

Christianity is not a religion. It is a relationship; a relationship with the one and only true God—the God who sent His one and only Son to die for us. Religion is a bunch of rules and regulations and traditions and yuck. Religion doesn't work. It only relies on you and your works and what you can do and not grace. It leaves you feeling frustrated with yourself because you know you can never be good enough. In Christianity, you realize that it is impossible to be good enough, or earn your way to heaven, so you have to completely and wholly trust and rely on God and put faith in Him and His Word. —SPENCER, AGE 15

3. What is it like to go from a condemned sinner to a child of God?

Going from a sinner of this world to a child of God is like nothing else you've ever experienced. When God speaks to you and deals with your heart, and you listen to Him and give your heart and life completely to God, it's like a huge weight being lifted off your shoulders. I've felt the weights of sin. But Jesus Christ took away all of my burdens. Now, I'm a free child of the King! No more pain from sin. God erased it all and put it under the blood so I don't have to live with my past any longer. —KAILEE, AGE 17

4. What advice would you give a new Christian in kicking off their relationship with God?

Constantly be in prayer. Always have an open heart to hear what God has for you. Always be willing to listen to people above you, whether it's your parents, pastor, teachers, etc. —HOLDEN, AGE 15

5. What are some of the most important (and/or effective) keys for evangelizing?

An effective key that I have found for evangelizing is to show interest or listen to what others have to say, and in that way, they will be more ready and willing to listen what you have to say, which, of course, is the Gospel! —HALEY, AGE 16

6. (In group discussion, for those who feel comfortable sharing) What is your testimony?

ABOUT THE AUTHOR

Fifteen-year-old Marjorie Jackson is a girl with a growing love for the Lord, for His Word, and for people. She and her family live in the southern United States, where Marjorie enjoys taking piano and voice lessons, theater (preferably musical), drawing, talking, spending time with family and friends, blogging, and eating dessert, to name a few hobbies. She is homeschooled (and not the least bit unsocial, mind you) along with her four younger sisters by her mom, Analucia, who is a stay-at-home mom, as well as a JuicePlus+ distributor (ajackson.juiceplus.com). Marjorie interns with her dad, Greg, in his graphic design business, Thinkpen Design (*thinkpendesign.com*).

Read Marjorie's Blog

Marjorie's blog, *Everything Pretty Much*, is viewed internationally by readers in sixteen countries and counting. Marjorie updates it periodically, mostly with devotionals aimed at but not limited to young people. You can subscribe at her site to receive free email notifications: *http://marjoriejackson.wordpress.com.*

Contact Marjorie

You can contact Marjorie through her blog (see above) by sending her a message in the Contact section. Or, you can send her an e-mail: notestomarjorie@gmail.com. She loves to hear from you!

WWW.FACEBOOK.COM/THEGREATESTBOOKYOUVENEVERREAD

ACKNOWLEDGMENTS

First and Foremost...

First of all, I thank my Heavenly Father for His guidance in this book. God uses different tools to accomplish His projects. Before I would sit down at the laptop and write this book, I would pray, "Jesus, let the words that I write be *Your words*, and not just my own wisdom." He was faithful, as always, in providing words to write and stamina to continue. He even taught me as I wrote. I love You and thank You, Jesus, for helping me all the way through!

This book really was a group effort. Personally, I probably wouldn't have decided to write it on my own, so I owe the *existence* and *conception* of this book to my loving parents, Greg and Analucia Jackson, for giving me a healthy nudge to cultivate the gift of writing into something special for the glory of the Lord. I may have resisted a little at first, but I really owe you for pushing me on to meet deadlines and keep me moving at a good pace. Thank you for your advice, suggestions, input, feedback, and revisions to my manuscript. God gave me parents for a reason.

Thanks to all my family for your supportiveness, enthusiasm, and your contributions! Thank you to my sisters, Genevieve, Melody, Harmony, and Felicity for making life *never dull*. I know we've given each other plenty of opportunities to practice what we preach, and I know and pray that we will continue growing closer to the Lord as we grow closer to one another. I love y'all!

Last But Not Least...

Thank you to all the guys and girls who so graciously allowed me to interview them and quote them in the "Food for Thought" sections of this book. If you got interviewed, look for the chapter that I quoted you in! It was so much fun collecting your answers, and I appreciate your effort!

Thank you, Mrs. Holley Gerth, for your willingness to help and give your feedback and advice on all things book and publishing related!

Thank you to my former English tutor, Tessa Swehla, for your English expertise, editing, and advice to many of the chapters in this book. I honestly learned a lot about writing under your coaching!

Thank you to my Ecclesia writing teacher, Mrs. Jennifer Hutchins, for helping with some of the final editing and revising stages. Your feedback helped me and encouraged me greatly. I continue to grow as an author by being in your classes.

RECOMMENDATIONS

A, B, C'S (APOLOGETICS, BEHEMOTHS, AND CREATION)

- *www.answersingenesis.org* (Creationism & Apologetics articles)
- Article on Job dinosaurs (see chapter 6):
  www.answersingenesis.org/articles/cm/v19/n4/sea-monsters

BIBLE

- *www.biblegateway.com* (also available in the App Store)
- *Good and Evil* by Michael Pearl (graphic novel Bible)
- *www.bible.com* (also available in the App Store)

ENTERTAINMENT

- Adventures In Odyssey: *www.whitsend.org* (radio drama)
- Sherwood Pictures Movies
- *Time Changer* (movie)

EVANGELISM

- *www.kerusso.com* (Christian apparel)
- *www.livingwaters.com* (Gospel tracts)
- *Will Our Generation Speak?* by Grace Mally (book)

CPSIA information can be obtained at www.ICGtesting.com
Printed in the USA
LVOW12s0648261213

366890LV00009B/211/P